A Year Without Fear

by

Katherine Hilditch

'A Year Without Fear'
by Katherine Hilditch

ISBN: 979-8-5587-5154-3

All Scripture quotations are taken from
the World English Bible British Edition (WEBBE)
unless marked KJV (King James Version)

CONTENTS

January 1st

Somewhere to start

When Jesus therefore had received the vinegar, he said, "It is finished!" Then he bowed his head and gave up his spirit.
(John 19:30)

We start with "It is finished!" Jesus said these words hanging on the Cross when He had won the victory over anything and everything that could come against us or try to hold us captive. And when it was all done, He announced, "It is finished!" He then did not wait for the cross to kill Him, but gave up His spirit when He knew He had completed the victory.

And so now it is possible for us to be free of everything negative including fear. We can start to live free from fear when we know and believe that Jesus finished the work God sent Him to do. We start from the finishing post not the starting line. Hallelujah!

January 2nd

<u>Something to grasp</u>

For God so loved the world, that he gave his only born Son, that whoever believes in him should not perish, but have eternal life.

(John 3:16)

What can be more wonderful or reassuring than to know that God loves you. If Almighty God who made the world and holds it all in His hand loves you, then what can you possibly fear. Think about it. Remind yourself of it through the day. Say it out loud – "God loves me." Let it settle in your mind and in your heart, and decide today that you are never going to doubt it, no matter what is said or what happens.

JANUARY 3RD

Something to take hold of

The Lord is not slow concerning his promise, as some count slowness; but he is patient with us, not wishing that anyone should perish, but that all should come to repentance.

(2 Peter 3:9)

Do you ever feel that God may love everyone else, but He can't possibly love you? You are not alone. I have heard many people say this. But know today that it is not true. This verse should allay your fears.

He does not want anyone to perish. That means He does not want you to perish, no matter what you've done and not done. And He wants everyone to be saved and spend eternity with Him in love, joy and peace. That means He wants to save you, regardless of what is going on in your life. Refuse to listen to fear. Instead, thank God that He loves you so much and turn to Him.

JANUARY 4TH

Something to know

"I am the way, the truth, and the life. No one comes to the Father, except through me."
(John 14:6)

The world is full of people saying all sorts of things, but there is only one person who has the whole truth and nothing but the truth – Jesus. Only He can take you to Father God and give you a life worth living in this world and in the next.

Take hold of Him and let Him show you the way, reveal truth to you and give you eternal life. Only in Him can you truly live a life free from fear.

JANUARY 5TH

Something to act upon

If you will confess with your mouth that Jesus is Lord and believe in your heart that God raised him from the dead, you will be saved. [10] For with the heart one believes resulting in righteousness; and with the mouth confession is made resulting in salvation. [11] For the Scripture says, "Whoever believes in him will not be disappointed."

(Romans 10:9-11)

To find eternal life with God you have to accept Jesus as your Lord and Saviour – He is the only way. Do it now sincerely and you will be born-again as a new creation in Jesus. You will step into a wonderful love relationship with your Father God and you will be able to start to live free from fear.

JANUARY 6TH

Something to understand

"You will know the truth, and the truth will make you free."

(John 8:32)

Only the truth can make you free from fear and the truth is only fully found in Jesus. Decide to learn the truth from Jesus in His Word, the Bible, and you can start to defeat fear in your life.

JANUARY 7TH

Something more to understand

"If therefore the Son makes you free, you will be free indeed."

(John 8:36)

When Jesus sets you free you are free indeed. The job is done – Jesus completed it as He died on the Cross. All you have to do is believe it, accept it and determine to walk forward in that freedom. Because of Jesus it is possible for you to be free from anything and everything that would come against you, including fear.

JANUARY 8TH

Something to realise

"I have loved you with an everlasting love. Therefore I have drawn you with loving kindness."
(Jeremiah 31:3)

This is the Lord God telling you of His everlasting love for you. He will never force you to love Him in return but He is always drawing you to Himself, longing for you to come to Him through Jesus. There is nothing you could do which would make God love you more because His love for you is already infinite. And there is nothing you can do which would make God love you less because His love for you is totally unconditional.

Allow His perfect love to bathe you and melt away your fears.

JANUARY 9TH

Something to take hold of

There is no fear in love; but perfect love casts out fear.
(1 John 4:18)

When you start to understand and experience just how much God loves you and how perfect and unfailing and unchanging His love is, it will become harder to be afraid. Go back to yesterday and speak God's words to you out loud – do it regularly. Say, "God loves me with an everlasting love. He is drawing me with loving-kindness. Thank You Lord – I receive your love."

Feed on His love and allow it to cast out your fear. Only God's perfect love can get rid of fear at its root.

JANUARY 10TH

Something to understand

For however many are the promises of God, in him is the "Yes." Therefore also through him is the "Amen", to the glory of God through us.

(2 Corinthians 1:20)

Every promise of God you can find in the Bible, both Old and New Testaments, has been stamped by Jesus as yours. Because of the victory He won for you through His death and resurrection they are all available to you. But you have to believe them and receive them.

When the Bible says that perfect love casts out fear, Jesus has stamped that 'Yes' and 'Amen' for you. Believe it and receive it and refuse to be side-tracked from it.

JANUARY 11TH

Something to never forget

For I am persuaded that neither death, nor life, nor angels, nor principalities, nor things present, nor things to come, nor powers, [39] nor height, nor depth, nor any other created thing will be able to separate us from God's love which is in Christ Jesus our Lord.

(Romans 8:38-39)

Be persuaded of God's unconditional love for you and make this your own declaration. Build yourself up in it. Fear has no place in the truth of this.

January 12th

Something to hold onto

"Behold, I am with you always, even to the end of the age."
(Matthew 28:20)

This is one of the many wonderful promises Jesus has made. He will never leave those who belong to Him – who are born-again. When He returned to heaven after His resurrection, Jesus sent His Holy Spirit to live in everyone who has made Him their Lord and Saviour. If that is you, be assured that you will never be alone again. When you have the love and power of Jesus living in you, why should you continue in fear? He is always with you – hallelujah!

JANUARY 13TH

Something to declare

So that with good courage we say, "The Lord is my helper. I will not fear. What can man do to me?"
(Hebrews 13:6)

With God on your side, helping you in everything you face, there is no room for fear. Decide to see the threats of men and negative situations as insignificant beside the love of God and His help. Declare this verse out loud with good courage. Don't say it tentatively or weakly but speak it out with a strong voice. It is the truth.

JANUARY 14TH

Something to build you up

For God didn't give us a spirit of fear, but of power, love, and self-control.
(2 Timothy 1:7)

Remember, God has made everything you need for this life available to you, and that includes the power and love of Jesus and the ability to control the decisions you make and the attitudes you live by. And God makes it very clear what He didn't give you – fear.

When you are fearful or anxious, know that it doesn't come from God. It is the devil who wants you to be crippled and limited by fear. Say 'No.' Focus instead on the love and power of Jesus and the self-control that is in you. They're there even if you can't feel them. Believe they are in you by faith, refuse to listen to fear, and start to experience His love and power in every area of your life.

JANUARY 15TH

Something to put into practice

Finally, brothers, whatever things are true, whatever things are honourable, whatever things are just, whatever things are pure, whatever things are lovely, whatever things are of good report: if there is any virtue and if there is anything worthy of praise, think about these things. [9] Do the things which you learnt, received, heard, and saw in me, and the God of peace will be with you.

(Philippians 4:8-9)

Do you want to have real peace in your mind and heart? I imagine most of us would answer "Yes" to that question. Philippians 4:4-9 tells us how we can. Paul tells us to rejoice in the Lord and not be anxious about anything, but ask God for what we need, thanking Him for it before we see it.

He then comes to today's verse which describes the kind of things we should be thinking about for God's peace to be able to fill us. We all know that the more we dwell on and talk about negative things, the less peace we feel and the more anxious and fearful we become. Instead, choose to dwell on things described in this list. Not only will you feel better, but you will also know God's special kind of peace which can remain no matter what is going on around you. I'm not saying it's easy, but the more you do it, the easier it becomes, and your default reaction to problems will start to change from one of fear to one of trust in God and a good outcome.

Think about such things as these, meditating on them and, using your imagination, see them in your life – fear will be silenced and the God of peace will be with you.

JANUARY 16TH

Something to understand

For though we walk in the flesh, we don't wage war according to the flesh; [4] for the weapons of our warfare are not of the flesh, but mighty before God to the throwing down of strongholds, [5] throwing down imaginations and every high thing that is exalted against the knowledge of God and bringing every thought into captivity to the obedience of Christ.

(2 Corinthians 10:3-5)

This is something we all really must get our heads round. When things are going against us, the devil is trying to wear us down, to divert us from what God wants for us and ultimately to get us to doubt our faith in Him. But he can only affect us to the extent that we let him. The battle is won or lost in our minds.

When we are afraid, our imagination can run riot. Throw such imaginations down and bring fearful thoughts into captivity. Say out loud with authority, "No! I'm not listening. I belong to Jesus and He has won every battle for me." Then replace them with the truth of God's Word. Start praising God and thanking Him for His victory in Jesus. Thank Him that He is going to lead you through everything you have to face and out the other side. In your imagination, now see yourself safely through it all, standing secure in Jesus.

Determine today that you are not going to listen to the devil's thoughts but instead, stand on the truth of God's Word. It might be a struggle at first, but the more you do it the easier it will become. Keep going and fear will be defeated. Thank You Lord!

January 17th

Something to live by

"The thief only comes to steal, kill, and destroy. I came that they may have life, and may have it abundantly."
(John 10:10)

So how do we know what is from God and what is from the devil? This is the verse I use all the time to answer that question. If something done or said is trying to steal something from you such as your health, or kill something such as your trust in God, or destroy something such as a good relationship, then it is from the devil. And any thoughts that come into your mind which are along the same lines are from the devil. But anything that is promising abundant life, such as health, joy in good things, provision, faith is from Jesus. Resist the first and take hold of the second.

Use this verse to help you see what is really going on in the things that happen to you, in what is said to you, and in your own thoughts and words.

JANUARY 18TH

Something to determine

"Haven't I commanded you? Be strong and courageous. Don't be afraid. Don't be dismayed, for the LORD your God is with you wherever you go."
(Joshua 1:9)

God had told Joshua to lead His people into the land He had promised was theirs. They were going to face enemies and difficult situations, but God commanded him to be strong in his thinking and emotions, and to be courageous as He set out to do what He had told him to do. God never commands us to do anything we can't do, however difficult it might seem. If God commands it, then it's possible. And He told Joshua not to be afraid or dismayed as he looked at all that was ahead. He then gave him the wonderful promise that He would be with Him wherever he went.

We can face all kinds of difficult situations too but God is always with us. When God shows you the way through difficult things, don't then continue to fear. Be strong instead and go forward with courage, not in your own strength or ability to somehow manage, but in God's power and ability to lead you through and out the other side.

January 19th

Something to remember

"Don't be afraid, little flock, for it is your Father's good pleasure to give you the Kingdom."
(Luke 12:32)

Just like Joshua yesterday, God has a land for you to live in – His Kingdom. And He wants you in it. you! No matter what you've done or haven't done, God loves you and wants you to be in His Kingdom in this life and forever after you die. Your being part of it will give Him such great pleasure. So don't be afraid – think about the wonderful Kingdom of God and praise Him for it. Take pleasure in it just like God does – it's what He wants for you.

JANUARY 20TH

Something to obey

Don't be conformed to this world, but be transformed by the renewing of your mind, so that you may prove what is the good, well-pleasing, and perfect will of God.
(Romans 12:2)

Maybe you feel totally inadequate to be part of God's Kingdom. Maybe you know you are part of it, but want to change and be more like Jesus. Maybe you find yourself fearful when you see all that is going on in the world and aren't sure how you should respond as a Christian. Take heart – there is an answer. Yes, you can be transformed. But it's not a question of asking God to change you and waiting for Him to do so. No, He's given us the responsibility. He tells us to be transformed by renewing our thinking and bringing it into line with His.

If you want to change, then get into God's Word and see the truth of all His promises for you, of all Jesus has done and won for you, of who you really are now you belong to Jesus. Meditate on it, speak it out loud and start to apply it in your everyday life. God promises that as you do so, He will indeed change you from glory into glory. Start the exciting journey today and see what a difference it makes and how fear is silenced as you replace it with the truth.

January 21st

Something to take hold of

Therefore if anyone is in Christ, he is a new creation. The old things have passed away. Behold, all things have become new.

(2 Corinthians 5:17)

This verse used to puzzle me so much. We used to often sing a song in church which began with the words 'I am a new creation'. As I sang it, I would say to God, "I know this is true because it says so in Your Word, but I don't understand it – I know myself too well." Then one day I learnt that it is my spirit which was instantly made a new perfect creation when I was born-again, not my body or my soul. It was a real lightbulb moment. I understood at last and now I could sing that song with real joy and confidence.

If you are born-again then your spirit has been exchanged for a brand new one – perfect just like Jesus. Wow! Think of that when you're next tempted to fear. Say out loud, "I am a new creation and fear has no part of me."

January 22nd

Something to know

But we have Christ's mind.
(1 Corinthians 2:16)

Really? As a Christian, do I really have the mind of Christ? Surely, if I did then I wouldn't think wrong thoughts sometimes. I would never fear. God's Word says that we do have Christ's mind so it is true, but how can that be? Remember from yesterday, it is your spirit, not your mind, that is perfect and so it is in your spirit that you have the mind of Christ. This means that all God's truth and wisdom is in you.

Get into God's Word and find it so you can draw it from your spirit into your own thinking. It is then that your human mind can start to be more like Jesus's and you can defeat fear before it takes hold. Thank You Jesus.

JANUARY 23RD

Something to take on board

Samuel said to the people, "Don't be afraid. You have indeed done all this evil; yet don't turn away from following the LORD, but serve the LORD with all your heart. [21] Don't turn away to go after vain things which can't profit or deliver, for they are vain. [22] For the LORD will not forsake his people for his great name's sake, because it has pleased the LORD to make you a people for himself."
(1 Samuel 12:20-22)

You may be struggling with all this talk of perfection. We all do and say and think wrong things, but you may be particularly aware of where you have got it wrong. Samuel spoke to the people about this. He didn't pretend that they hadn't done evil, but he told them not to let what they'd done in the past stop them from following God now. He warned them against turning to other ways and means to try and get to heaven. There is no other – only Jesus.

When we turn to Jesus, we have His promise that we will be His forever. So don't be fearful about what you've done, however big it may be. Turn to Jesus and receive the forgiveness He has won for you on the Cross and keep your focus on Him and Him alone. God is on your side.

JANUARY 24TH

<u>Something to put into practice</u>

For God didn't appoint us to wrath, but to the obtaining of salvation through our Lord Jesus Christ, [10] who died for us, that, whether we wake or sleep, we should live together with him. [11] Therefore exhort one another, and build each other up, even as you also do.

(1 Thessalonians 5:9-11)

God isn't angry with us. He put all the punishment we deserve on Jesus and He suffered it in our place so we can walk free from guilt and shame. God's desire isn't that we live in fear of His anger, but that we accept and believe the forgiveness and salvation Jesus has won for us. And this verse tells us not only to believe it for ourselves, but to encourage others with this truth as well.

Refuse to believe the lie that God is angry with you. Instead rejoice in your forgiveness and salvation. And when you see other Christians fearful of God's anger, show them the truth so they can be built up in it just like you.

January 25th

Something to take hold of

There is therefore now no condemnation to those who are in Christ Jesus, who don't walk according to the flesh, but according to the Spirit.
(Romans 8:1)

This is the truth. When you belong to Jesus you are free of all condemnation. Sometimes, if we live in our own way instead of God's way, we will feel condemned but it never comes from God. Don't be afraid – you are not condemned by God. You are forgiven.

JANUARY 26TH

Something to act upon

Blessed is the man who doesn't walk in the counsel of the wicked, nor stand on the path of sinners, nor sit in the seat of scoffers; 2 but his delight is in the LORD's law. On his law he meditates day and night. 3 He will be like a tree planted by the streams of water, that produces its fruit in its season, whose leaf also does not wither. Whatever he does shall prosper.

(Psalm 1:1-3)

Base your life on the truth of God's Word – read it, meditate on it, let it reveal its truth to you and seek to live your life in its light; and instead of feeling fearful, you will find peace and blessing come your way.

JANUARY 27TH

<u>Something to take hold of</u>

Thus consider yourselves also to be dead to sin, but alive to God in Christ Jesus our Lord.
(Romans 6:11)

The Bible tells us that without Jesus we are all slaves to sin, but when you gave your life to Jesus, your old self died. You may have been basically good before you became a believer, but you know that you weren't perfect. Or sin may have played a large part in your life. Well, that old self was crucified with Jesus when you were born-again, and you were given a brand-new perfect spirit in its place. Although you will still sin, it no longer holds you – you can say "No" to it. Now you are drawn to live a life that is pleasing to God and you feel sorry when you have sinned.

You're not a sinner; not even a sinner saved by grace, as is so often said. You were a sinner; you were then saved by grace and now you are a saint. Nowhere in the Bible is a believer called a sinner; they are called saints. We still sin sometimes but it no longer defines who we are. We are defined by the righteousness we have from Jesus.

Take hold of this and consider yourself dead to sin. This doesn't mean sin doesn't matter – it does. It will hurt you and others around you, and it will give the devil an inroad into your life. But none of us live perfectly, so when you do sin, repent quickly and receive your forgiveness. Don't allow yourself to get into self-condemnation and fear. You used to be dead to Christ and alive to sin. Thank God that you are now dead to sin and alive to Christ. Walk forward rejoicing that you are now a saint.

January 28th

<u>Something to put into practice</u>

He who dwells in the secret place of the Most High will rest in the shadow of the Almighty. [2] I will say of the LORD, "He is my refuge and my fortress; my God, in whom I trust."
(Psalm 91:1-2)

Today we start to look at Psalm 91. It is a wonderful psalm full of God's promises for His people. They aren't just for others – they're for you, as long as you meet the conditions in these first two verses. I don't say this to make you feel inadequate in any way. I say it because it is in God's Word and it is the means for you to be able to face the world with confidence and all that it might try and throw at you. I want to encourage you and build you up in Jesus.

Remember the verse for January 25th and take heart. Live your life in relationship with God, not just in religious observance and you will find yourself under His shadow – under His protection. And speak your trust in Him out loud. Then all the following promises can be reality in your life. Fear will have no place. Don't do yourself down or compare yourself with others. Just look to Jesus and you can walk in all the promises that follow and turn away from fear.

January 29th

Something to grasp

For he will deliver you from the snare of the fowler, and from the deadly pestilence.

(Psalm 91:3)

God will protect you from sudden traps of the enemy and from deadly diseases like COVID 19. If you live in relationship with God as your Father and you as His child this wonderful promise is for you. But like all God's promises, you have to believe it and take hold of it. Declaring it out loud will help it to take root in your mind and in your emotions and it can then drive out any fear associated with harm and serious illness.

JANUARY 30TH

Something to understand

He will cover you with his feathers. Under his wings you will take refuge.
(Psalm 91:4)

This is a picture for those of us who live in relationship with God as our Father. He covers us with His feathers just like a mother bird does with her chicks. And that is a place of refuge – safety from all threats. Who could fear when they really know God Himself is covering them and keeping them safe?

January 31st

Something to take hold of

His faithfulness is your shield and rampart.
(Psalm 91:4)

The God who is protecting you is faithful – He will never let you down. He will protect you against all attacks just like a shield stops weapons from hitting you. And He provides you with a fortified place, a rampart, from which you can safely attack back with the truth of God's Word.

February 1st

Something to determine

You shall not be afraid of the terror by night, nor of the arrow that flies by day ...
(Psalm 91:5)

We continue reading through Psalm 91.

What a wonderful promise in this verse – to not be afraid of terror in the night or of things that fly at us in the day. We know how awful things can seem in the middle of the night and the shock of something taking us unawares in the daytime. But it is possible for you to live free from the fear of them when you are in relationship with God through Jesus.

As you set your mind and your heart on the love God has for you, and come under His wings of protection, you will be able to know peace not fear.

February 2nd

<u>Something to realise</u>

... nor of the pestilence that walks in darkness, nor of the destruction that wastes at noonday.

(Psalm 91:6)

This talks of night and day again. God promises to protect us all the time from things we can't see, such as disease, when we live in true relationship with Him, declaring our trust in Him as described in verses 1-2.

FEBRUARY 3RD

Something to take on board

A thousand may fall at your side, and ten thousand at your right hand; but it will not come near you. [8] You will only look with your eyes, and see the recompense of the wicked.

(Psalm 91:7-8)

People may be dying of disease all around us but if our trust is truly in God and His promises then we will be safe. It sounds too good to be true but it is in God's Word and if you refuse to believe it, then you can't trust anything else God says.

Decide to believe it today no matter what is happening to you or around you. Enter fully into the love relationship God has for you and declare your trust in Him and His promises. Say out loud with authority, "He is my refuge and my fortress; my God, in whom I trust." (verse 2)

FEBRUARY 4TH

Something to enjoy

Because you have made the LORD your refuge, and the Most High your dwelling place, [10] no evil shall happen to you ...

(Psalm 91:9-10)

Today we are halfway through Psalm 91 and this verse reminds us of the conditions we need to fulfil to be able to see all these wonderful promises of God's protection realised in our lives. We need to make God our refuge, knowing we are safe with Him, and living in relationship with Him, not just going through the motions. Our life with Him and in Him must be sincere and needs to be our foundation. Then we can say with faith, "No evil shall happen to me." When we get to the place where we are fully convinced of this, then there is no place for fear.

February 5th

Something to rejoice about

... neither shall any plague come near your dwelling.
(Psalm 91:10)

What a promise for today as we live in the middle of the COVID 19 pandemic. There have been many pandemics before – think of the plague and the Spanish flu and many others which have killed thousands of people over the centuries. Your dwelling in this verse does not mean your house but your body. Many Christians must have stood on this promise in the past and seen it become reality for them.

Be one of those today as you dwell in relationship with God and declare that neither COVID 19 nor any other pandemic can touch your body and live. Speak out loud with authority, "In the name of Jesus I declare that any disease germ or virus that touches my body will instantly die. Thank You Lord."

FEBRUARY 6TH

Something to know

For he will put his angels in charge of you, to guard you in all your ways. [12] They will bear you up in their hands, so that you won't dash your foot against a stone.
(Psalm 91:11-12)

Isn't this wonderful! God uses His angels to save us when we might hurt ourselves. I look back on times in my life when I could so easily have been hurt through some kind of accident but somehow it didn't happen or I wasn't hurt by it. And I remember other times when I was injured. I now know that if I am living under God's protection in relationship with Him, that I can trust His angels to save me from harm.

This doesn't mean that we can be reckless. We should not put God to the test. If we decide to jump off a cliff on purpose, then we will face the consequences. But if we fall by accident then we can trust this promise. Choose to believe it and refuse to fear accidents.

February 7th

<u>Something to take hold of</u>

You will tread on the lion and cobra. You will trample the young lion and the serpent underfoot.
(Psalm 91:13)

When you are living in relationship with God and declaring your sincere trust in Him, you do not need to fear potentially deadly situations. God promises to save you from them. Again, this does not mean that you can put God to the test and recklessly do deadly things. But if you find yourself in such a situation, stand on this promise. God is good and God is faithful and God is able to protect and save you.

February 8th

<u>Something to rejoice about</u>

"Because he has set his love on me, therefore I will deliver him."

(Psalm 91:14)

We are now on day 12 of Psalm 91. What wonderful promises this psalm has for us. Here God Himself starts to speak and explains further the necessary conditions to be able to walk in their fulfilment. He says that we need to set our love on Him. This isn't talking about a feeling of love which can come and go, but a decision to set our love on Him. To set is to firmly place your love on Him and leave it there. When you have truly done this, then you will love Him no matter what.

When you know you are perfectly loved by God and that you have set your love on Him, you have nothing to fear. You will know that He will deliver you from anything and everything that would try to come against you.

February 9th

Something to grasp

"I will set him on high, because he has known my name."
(Psalm 91:14)

And here is one last condition – that you have known the name of God and of your Saviour, Jesus. You know that it is God and God alone who can save you and that it is only through Jesus that it is possible. When you recognise the name of Jesus as the Name above all names then God sets you on high with Him. In your spirit you are seated with Him far above all fear and anxiety, and all the following promises are yours.

FEBRUARY 10TH

Something to act upon

"He will call on me, and I will answer him."
(Psalm 91:15)

Here is the first of six things God will do for you when you have known His name and set your love on Him.

When you call on Him in the name of Jesus, He will answer you. Believe it. God always hears your prayers even when it may seem otherwise. Refuse to trust your feelings, instead choose to trust His Word. Thank Him that He has heard you and trust Him to answer you and get that answer to you. When you have placed your cares on Jesus do not fear – wait in faith.

FEBRUARY 11TH

Something to rejoice about

"I will be with him in trouble. I will deliver him, and honour him."

(Psalm 91:15)

Now we find three more promises. God will be with you in any and every trouble you face. That has to make a difference. If God Almighty is with You then why should you fear. He will deliver you out of trouble and He will honour you. Why would God honour us? Not because we have earned it or deserve it, but because we have honoured Him by believing in Him and living in a true relationship with Him. What a wonder to be honoured by God – off you go fear – you have no place in me.

FEBRUARY 12TH

Something to enjoy

"I will satisfy him with long life, and show him my salvation."

(Psalm 91:16)

And so we come to the last verse of Psalm 91 with two final promises. First, God will satisfy us with long life – our life won't be cut short, rather we will die at the end of a satisfied life. And second, we find our salvation here and now through Jesus but when we eventually die, if Jesus doesn't return first, we will find the fulfilment of that salvation as we go to live with God forever. What a great way to end this psalm – looking forward to a life of perfect love, peace and joy with Jesus, free from all pain and trouble. The things we worry about and fear on earth pale into insignificance against the glory of heaven.

I'm not belittling the real troubles that you go through – I'm trying to turn your attention to what will last forever in order to encourage you and help you to live your life on this earth free from fear. God will help you meet the conditions of this psalm if you sincerely ask Him.

Don't strive and don't allow yourself or others or circumstances to condemn you. Walk forward with Jesus in His truth and you will find it gets easier day by day. Make today the day you start and you will never regret it.

FEBRUARY 13TH

Something to know

But God, being rich in mercy, for his great love with which he loved us, [5] even when we were dead through our trespasses, made us alive together with Christ — by grace you have been saved — [6] and raised us up with him, and made us to sit with him in the heavenly places in Christ Jesus, [7] that in the ages to come he might show the exceeding riches of his grace in kindness towards us in Christ Jesus.

(Ephesians 2:4-7)

Here is a description of how and where we are raised up by God. Look back at February 9th. Because of His great unconditional love for us and His mercy, shown to us through Jesus, our born-again spirits are already seated with God in heaven. Wow! God loves you so much. He longs to shower you with His love and mercy and grace and kindness. That's how special you are. Don't let fear rob you of the way God sees you and where you are seated in Him.

February 14th

Something to choose

I call heaven and earth to witness against you today that I have set before you life and death, the blessing and the curse. Therefore choose life, that you may live.
(Deuteronomy 30:19)

After the Israelites came out of slavery in Egypt, God gave them the law. It wasn't so that they could earn their salvation by obeying it. The law was so detailed, it was impossible to keep it all perfectly. God gave it to show them that His perfection is impossibly high for anyone to reach in their own strength. He wanted them to realise that they needed a Saviour. The law paved the way for Jesus.

God told the people that if they kept the law they would be blessed and if they broke it they would be cursed. Living God's way led to life and living their own way led to death. That may not have been instant physical death, but it was certainly a spiritual death.

Jesus won the victory over all sin on the Cross, so there is now no fear of punishment for those who know Jesus. But living God's way still brings life and, even though our sin doesn't break our relationship with God, living our own way and opens the door to all sorts of things including fear.

God gave a choice to the Israelites. He described the two ways of living and then, to make it really obvious, He told them which was the right way. He says the same to us today, "I have set before you life and death ... choose life." Which will you choose? Security in Jesus living God's way or fear, doing it your own way. Be encouraged – choose life.

FEBRUARY 15TH

Something to understand

For God didn't send his Son into the world to judge the world, but that the world should be saved through him. [18] He who believes in him is not judged. He who doesn't believe has been judged already, because he has not believed in the name of the only born Son of God.
(John 3:17-18)

Because God judged people under the law in the Old Testament, many today think that He is waiting to pounce on them if they get anything wrong. That is so far from the truth. God didn't send Jesus to earth to judge us, but to save us. It was all motivated by His unconditional love and mercy.

However, when Jesus comes again, He will judge the world then. But not in the way most people would imagine. He won't judge us for all our sins. He will judge us for just one – have we believed in His name or have we rejected Him? For those who have believed in Him there is no judgement. But those who have rejected Him will be sent to eternal punishment, not because that's what God wants, but because that is what they have chosen. It will be too late then for them to change their mind. The Bible says that God doesn't want any to perish but many will do so of their own free will.

If you are born-again, you have nothing to fear of God. When the devil whispers in your ear of things you've done wrong, tell him you're not listening – you're on your way to heaven and he is on his way to hell. Don't let him put fear in your heart. With God there is peace and joy and love forever and ever. What a future!

FEBRUARY 16TH

Something to remember

He said to his disciples, "Therefore I tell you, don't be anxious for your life, what you will eat, nor yet for your body, what you will wear. [23] Life is more than food, and the body is more than clothing. [24] Consider the ravens: they don't sow, they don't reap, they have no warehouse or barn, and God feeds them. How much more valuable are you than birds!"

(Luke 12:22-24)

Sometimes it isn't the big things that make us anxious – sometimes it's the everyday concerns, such as how we are going to feed and clothe ourselves and our families.

Jesus explains to His disciples and us that the birds don't worry about whether they'll have enough to eat or not – God provides what they need.

He isn't saying we don't need to plan menus, shop for food or prepare it. He's saying that we don't need to worry about it. God knows we need food and if we trust Him, He will make sure we have enough.

FEBRUARY 17TH

Something else to remember

"Which of you by being anxious can add a cubit to his height? [26] If then you aren't able to do even the least things, why are you anxious about the rest? [27] Consider the lilies, how they grow. They don't toil, neither do they spin; yet I tell you, even Solomon in all his glory was not arrayed like one of these. [28] But if this is how God clothes the grass in the field, which today exists and tomorrow is cast into the oven, how much more will he clothe you, O you of little faith?"

(Luke 12:25-28)

Jesus then tells us not to worry about clothes. He who made all the beauty of the world is well able to provide for our needs. Again, He isn't saying that we shouldn't enjoy shopping for clothes – He's telling us not to be anxious about it.

Worrying about these things will never change anything. Decide today that you are going to trust Him for your everyday needs and you will find your faith rise and anxiety recede.

FEBRUARY 18TH

Something to obey

"Therefore don't be anxious, saying, 'What will we eat?',
'What will we drink?' or, 'With what will we be clothed?'
32 For the Gentiles seek after all these things; for your
heavenly Father knows that you need all these things.
33 But seek first God's Kingdom and his righteousness; and
all these things will be given to you as well."
(Matthew 6:31-33)

Jesus then goes on to say that it's when we put God first and make all that Jesus has done and won for us our priority, that our everyday needs will be met. So instead of being anxious about what to eat or wear, say, "How can I seek God and do what He wants me to do today?" As you see your needs being met you will realise there was no point in being anxious at all. As Jesus said in yesterday's verse, worry can never improve anything. It can only sap your strength which makes things even harder. Take hold of this promise and see it come to pass.

FEBRUARY 19TH

Something to understand

Jesus said to him, "If you can believe, all things are possible to him who believes." [24] Immediately the father of the child cried out with tears, "I believe. Help my unbelief!"
(Mark 9:23-24)

The man Jesus was talking to had a son with a demon and he wanted Jesus to get rid of the demon so his son could live a normal life. Jesus told him that his faith was the important factor.

Imagine a thermometer with faith at the top and unbelief at the bottom – we think that we register somewhere between the two extremes and the point varies according to how we feel. But this man knew something very significant – he knew that both faith and unbelief could exist at the same time. Instead of one thermometer, we have two. One is called faith and we can register anywhere on it and the other is called unbelief and we can register anywhere on that too. So it's possible to have lots of faith and lots of unbelief at the same time. The problem is that unbelief cancels out faith.

This man knew he had faith but he knew he had unbelief too and he was fearful. So he didn't ask Jesus to help him increase his faith; he asked Him to help him get rid of his unbelief.

This is what our attitude should be. When we knock unbelief on the head by applying the truth of God's Word, then anything is possible. Instead of being fearful, deal with your unbelief and know that your faith in Jesus, however small, is enough for God to work.

February 20th

Something to act upon

Jesus answered them, "Have faith in God. [23] For most certainly I tell you, whoever may tell this mountain, 'Be taken up and cast into the sea,' and doesn't doubt in his heart, but believes that what he says is happening, he shall have whatever he says."

(Mark 11:22-23)

What a statement! But it's Jesus who made it and it is therefore true. Mountains are problems in your life; they may be small or they may be huge, but any size mountain can cause you to be fearful. Choose to believe what Jesus says and command the mountain to go in the name of Jesus with faith, then it must go. It may take time, but persevere because the Word of Jesus is always true.

In Matthew's account of the same conversation, Jesus says that you only need faith the size of a mustard seed – that's small. So if you feel your faith isn't enough, don't worry. Just refuse to think negative thoughts of unbelief – remember, you only need a small amount of faith as long as no doubt or unbelief cancels it out.

FEBRUARY 21ST

Something to take hold of

"Therefore I tell you, all things whatever you pray and ask for, believe that you have received them, and you shall have them."

(Mark 11:24)

Jesus continues to talk to His disciples about faith, relating it to prayer. When you ask God for something you know is part of His will for you, use your imagination to believe it is already yours and it will be. If you are fearful of God not answering or not giving you what you've asked for, then you do not believe it is already yours. Turn away from fear because it will not help and will in fact hinder the answer to your prayer. Choose Jesus over fear – He's already won the victory over it for you.

February 22nd

Something to determine

Jesus spoke to them, saying "Cheer up! It is I! Don't be afraid." 28 Peter answered him and said, "Lord, if it is you, command me to come to you on the waters." 29 He said, "Come!" Peter stepped down from the boat and walked on the waters to come to Jesus. 30 But when he saw that the wind was strong, he was afraid, and beginning to sink, he cried out, saying, "Lord, save me!" 31 Immediately Jesus stretched out his hand, took hold of him, and said to him, "You of little faith, why did you doubt?"
(Matthew 14:27-31)

There was a storm and the disciples were in trouble in their boat, so Jesus came walking on the water to help and encourage them. Peter knew he could do the same if Jesus asked him to. And he could – he walked on the storm-tossed sea. But then he looked at the waves and the wind, and suddenly he began to doubt and started to sink. He took his eyes off Jesus and the fact that He had told him to come to Him, and looked at his circumstances instead. Fear rose in him and unbelief took over.

When you're going through a storm, keep your eyes on Jesus. If you start focusing on what's going on, fear will come in. Jesus said to Peter, "Why did you doubt?" It's a good question considering that Jesus Himself was there. Jesus is there with you too. Call out to Him when things are difficult and He will immediately take hold of you and bring you to safety – there is no need to fear; it only makes things worse. It is faith, however small, which is not cancelled out by doubt, that keeps us on top of the storm.

FEBRUARY 23RD

Something to remember

Many are the afflictions of the righteous, but the LORD delivers him out of them all.

(Psalm 34:19)

God has never promised us a life free of problems and trouble, but He has promised us that when we look to Him in faith and do not doubt, that He will bring us through them. And not just a few of them or some or even the majority, but ALL. When you are afflicted in some way, say no to fear and yes to God's promise and see how He will deliver you.

FEBRUARY 24TH

<u>Something to obey</u>

"Be strong and courageous; for you shall cause this people to inherit the land which I swore to their fathers to give them. [7] Only be strong and very courageous. Be careful to observe to do according to all the law which Moses my servant commanded you. Don't turn from it to the right hand or to the left, that you may have good success wherever you go."

(Joshua 1:6-7)

Remember Joshua who led God's people into the promised land? He must have been so tempted to fear for God to keep telling him to be strong and courageous. Is that you? Do you turn away from fear, only to turn back to it? It's something that we have all had to deal with. God tells Joshua to do things His way according to His Word; to keep on His path and he would then have success.

When you're finding things difficult and keep being tempted to fear, go to God's Word and build yourself up in His truth and in His ways and in who you are in Him. Seek to live by it as you go through trouble. Refuse to be led off God's way and you will find success too.

FEBRUARY 25TH

Something to take hold of

"This book of the law shall not depart from your mouth, but you shall meditate on it day and night, that you may observe to do according to all that is written in it; for then you shall make your way prosperous, and then you shall have good success."

(Joshua 1:8)

God goes on to tell Joshua to keep meditating on His Word so that it becomes a part of him and the foundation on which he lives his life. He promises him that he will then prosper and be successful. Take hold of this promise for yourself. Read and think about God's Word and seek to live your life by it in thought, word and deed, and things will work out well for you too. Fear cannot stand against the truth of God.

FEBRUARY 26TH

Something to remember

Don't be afraid of sudden fear, neither of the desolation of the wicked, when it comes; [26] for the LORD will be your confidence, and will keep your foot from being taken.

(Proverbs 3:25-26)

Sometimes we can fear fear itself. What if it suddenly comes upon me and paralyses me? You are worrying about something before it even happens. Refuse to give fear that power. Put your confidence in the Lord and He will lead you through anything that happens, whether it comes upon you suddenly or gradually.

February 27th

Something to determine

But you be strong! Don't let your hands be slack, for your work will be rewarded.
(2 Chronicles 15:7)

When fear paralyses us it will stop us from doing what God has called us to do. Determine that you aren't going to let that happen. Keep doing the things that are pleasing to God knowing that what you do for God with a sincere heart will one day be rewarded – in the next life, if not in this.

February 28th

Something to hold onto

"No weapon that is formed against you will prevail; and you will condemn every tongue that rises against you in judgement. This is the heritage of the LORD's servants, and their righteousness is of me," says the LORD.

(Isaiah 54:17)

This is a verse I have learnt to hold onto. Whatever tries to come against me cannot succeed because I belong to God and am clothed in the righteousness of Jesus. But I have to play my part. I have to condemn words that are spoken against me. If someone says something hurtful or something negative about my future, I condemn the words (not the person) as soon as I can. I say something like, "I condemn those words about .... in the name of Jesus. I declare that they have no power to hurt or influence me in any way. Thank You Lord." Try it and you will find confidence in Jesus rise in your heart instead of fear at what was said.

February 29th

Something to realise

The LORD will command his loving kindness in the daytime. In the night his song shall be with me: a prayer to the God of my life.

(Psalm 42:8)

God's loving kindness never runs out – it is raining down upon you all day and all night. The result isn't a heart full of fear, but a heart singing praise and thanks to God. Remind yourself of this when things are difficult. Imagine God's love and kindness pouring over you and filling you and fear will have to go.

MARCH 1ST

Something to understand

Be strong, and let your heart take courage, all you who hope in the LORD.

(Psalm 31:24)

This is the same command that God gave to Joshua. Do you hope in the Lord? Do you put your trust and faith in Him for today and the future? It's a question we all need to face. Let's determine to be people who do hope in the Lord, then we can be strong in Him. God tells us to let our heart take courage. In other words, don't do or say or think negative things that would hinder that happening. Do all you can, by standing on God's truth, to encourage your heart to take courage.

MARCH 2ND

Something to declare

The LORD is on my side. I will not be afraid. What can man do to me?

(Psalm 118:6)

The Lord God Almighty who made the heavens and the earth is on my side. What more can I want! With that knowledge I can truly say, "I will not be afraid. What can man do to me?"

MARCH 3RD

Something to understand

Yes, and all who desire to live godly in Christ Jesus will suffer persecution.

(2 Timothy 3:12)

This is a verse we could wish wasn't in the Bible. But it is. We have seen over the previous days how God protects us from evil when we trust in Jesus. But there is one exception. Jesus did not win victory over persecution for our faith in Him.

It is believed that all the disciples except one, ended up being killed for their faith and down the ages, countless others have been tortured, made homeless, seen their families ripped apart or been killed for their belief in Jesus. If our faith in Jesus is real then this verse tells us we will suffer persecution too. It may not be so horrendous, but the sneer, the challenge, the avoidance, the refusal to listen etc are all forms of persecution. But remember, we never suffer it alone. Jesus suffers with us and will help us through it every time. There's some more good news tomorrow!

MARCH 4TH

Something to remember

"Blessed are those who have been persecuted for righteousness' sake, for theirs is the Kingdom of Heaven."
(Matthew 5:10)

Good news – when you are persecuted for your faith in Jesus you are blessed by God. You know that you are part of God's family and a member of His Kingdom. Focus on the blessing and not the fear of persecution. If it comes, God will bless you – He has promised.

MARCH 5TH

Something to rejoice in

But as many as received him, to them he gave the right to become God's children, to those who believe in his name: [13] who were born, not of blood, nor of the will of the flesh, nor of the will of man, but of God.

(John 1:12-13)

Rejoice that you are a child of God. No matter what happens to you, nothing can change that because you believe in the name of Jesus and have been born-again.

When fear starts to come in, tell it to go. Say, "Fear, you get out. I'm not listening to you. I am a child of God and you have no place in me and I deny you any influence in my life." Then start thanking and praising God for all His goodness and faithfulness and love.

MARCH 6TH

<u>Something to know</u>

Without faith it is impossible to be well pleasing to him, for he who comes to God must believe that he exists, and that he is a rewarder of those who seek him.

(Hebrews 11:6)

It's easy to believe in something you can see, but it takes faith to believe in something you can't. God looks for faith because then we are really trusting Him and His Word. Make sure you get your head round this. If you don't have faith, it doesn't matter how many good things you do, you cannot please God. God doesn't even say that it's difficult to please Him without faith; He says it is impossible. But don't let that make you fearful – instead, let it make you determined to build yourself up in God's Word so faith will rise and fear and doubt diminish. Take heart. Speak out your faith in Jesus and watch fear start to run.

MARCH 7TH

Something to take hold of

So faith comes by hearing, and hearing by the word of God.
(Romans 10:17)

Where does faith come from? It comes from God's Word. If you want to see your faith work, get rid of unbelief. You will only do this by getting into God's Word and taking it on board. This verse tells us that faith comes by hearing God's Word, so this might sound strange, but read it out loud so you hear it with your ears. It will penetrate your thinking more quickly and reach your heart more readily. The more you hear it the more your faith will rise. And the less you will be tempted to fear and unbelief.

MARCH 8TH

Something to encourage you

"Come to me, all you who labour and are heavily burdened, and I will give you rest. [29] Take my yoke upon you and learn from me, for I am gentle and humble in heart; and you will find rest for your souls. [30] For my yoke is easy, and my burden is light."

(Matthew 11:28-30)

These are Jesus's wonderful words to those who are weary and heavily burdened. We can be burdened in lots of different ways, but being anxious and afraid certainly weighs on us. Go to Jesus. Choose to trust in Him, in all He has done and won for you and in all His promises and allow Him to fill you with His rest and peace.

God has a plan for your life, but it is never meant to be heavy because He is with you, helping you all the way. Lay your fear and other heavy burdens down and walk forward in Jesus – easier and lighter.

MARCH 9TH

Something to decide

Return to your rest, my soul, for the LORD has dealt bountifully with you. [8] For you have delivered my soul from death, my eyes from tears, and my feet from falling. [9] I will walk before the LORD in the land of the living.

(Psalm 116:7-9)

I love this verse. It's so easy to get bogged down in fear, anxiety and negativity and suddenly realise that you aren't in Jesus's rest anymore. But it's easy to get back into it too. However, you have to make a decision to turn away from the negativity and fear and refocus on Jesus.

One way to help you is to remind yourself of all Jesus has done for you – He has delivered your thinking and your emotions from death; He has comforted you and dried your tears and He has saved you from falling in so many different ways – physically and spiritually. Make that decision today to live in Jesus's rest again and start enjoying life instead of being fearful.

MARCH 10TH

Something to remember

Death and life are in the power of the tongue; those who love it will eat its fruit.

(Proverbs 18:21)

This is such an important truth to get hold of and remember. Do you remember the old saying, 'Sticks and stones can break my bones but words will never hurt me.' It is not true. I'm sure you know as well as I do, that the things people say can really hurt. When we speak positive encouraging words, they are words of life and they build people up. But when we say negative words, they are death and will hurt others and that hurt can be great indeed.

What we say has consequences for ourselves as well as for other people. What you speak about yourself will be life or death too. When you say, "I can do this because Jesus will help me," you are speaking life. When you say, "I'll never be able to do this," you are speaking death. If you say negative things about yourself repeatedly, you will find your thought pattern becoming more and more negative and you will be able to accomplish less and less.

Don't be afraid of negative words; instead decide to start to train yourself to speak words that are life. Listen to what you say to others and about yourself. Speak the truth as God sees you – He has said that you can do all things through Him.

MARCH 11TH

Something to take hold of

"Be strong and courageous. Don't be afraid or scared of them, for the LORD your God himself is who goes with you. He will not fail you nor forsake you."

(Deuteronomy 31:6)

This is Moses speaking to God's people before Joshua led them into the promised land. He uses those same words which God would later speak to Joshua – "Be strong and courageous." How God wanted them to get this. He said to not be afraid of the people they would find there and who they would have to fight, because He was with them and had promised them victory. So often we look at the situation before us and start to fear because it looks daunting or impossible. We need to get our thoughts off what we can see, hear, smell, taste and feel and focus on God's promises instead.

When you look at what's going on and feel anxiety or fear, catch yourself before it takes root. God wants you to use your faith, not your five physical senses. Remind yourself of His promise to be with you and not fail you and walk forward in faith in Him. He will never let you down.

MARCH 12TH

Something to realise

Now to him who is able to do exceedingly abundantly above all that we ask or think, according to the power that works in us, [21] to him be the glory in the assembly and in Christ Jesus to all generations, forever and ever. Amen.
(Ephesians 3:20-21)

Isn't this wonderful – God is able to do far, far more than we can even imagine. But look at the next part of the sentence – He does it according to the power He has put in us. Yes, God has put His power in you if you are born-again. But notice it says 'according to the power'. It's not God's power that varies but how much we use it and allow it to work. Put fear aside today and step out in the power of God that is in you and see the amazing things God can do in you and through you.

MARCH 13TH

Something to reassure you

"For I know the thoughts that I think towards you," says the LORD, "thoughts of peace, and not of evil, to give you hope and a future."
(Jeremiah 29:11)

So often people blame God for the bad things that happen, but God is a good God. He doesn't want bad things to happen to you. He has a plan for your life and it's one for you to live in peace. It's not one that involves evil in any way. It's one to give you hope and a good future. What a loving heavenly Father. Don't be afraid of what God's plan might be for you. Thank Him that's it's good and set out to discover it and follow it. Exciting times ahead!

March 14th

Something to bless you

Blessed is the man who trusts in the LORD, and whose confidence is in the LORD. [8] For he will be as a tree planted by the waters, who spreads out its roots by the river, and will not fear when heat comes, but its leaf will be green, and will not be concerned in the year of drought. It won't cease from yielding fruit.

(Jeremiah 17:7-8)

This is a wonderful picture of the person who is in relationship with God and puts all His trust in Him. He is in a great position where He can feed on God's Word and has determined not to be afraid if conditions change for the worse. With His focus on God and His trust in Him He will still be safe and fruitful. Is that you or does this description leave you feeling inadequate and fearful? Get your focus on Jesus and choose to trust Him and God will do the rest.

MARCH 15TH

Something to declare

Be courageous, and let's be strong for our people and for the cities of our God.

(1 Chronicles 19:13)

These are words spoken by Joab before he led the Israelites into battle. He calls the soldiers to be courageous – brave and fearless. And he says to do this not only for themselves, but also for the rest of the Israelites who were to benefit from their victory. Is there someone you can encourage today by telling them to be courageous in the Lord? Maybe your words will help them to turn away from fear and step out in the things God is calling them to do.

MARCH 16TH

Something to take hold of

Happy is the man who finds wisdom, the man who gets understanding. [14] For her good profit is better than getting silver, and her return is better than fine gold. [15] She is more precious than rubies. None of the things you can desire are to be compared to her.

(Proverbs 3:13-15)

Today we are starting to look at six verses in Proverbs 3. They are all about God's wisdom and how taking hold of it and applying it in our lives will benefit us immensely.

Do you go to God's Word to find the direction for your life and guidance in how you do things along the way? Or do you listen to what the media says or to the advice of others or your own thoughts without assessing it by God's truth? Choose to find God's wisdom – seek Him and He will help you. Read His Word – you'll find His wisdom there. Then put it into practice in the big things and the little things of life. You will then be truly happy and the benefit that comes to you will be so much better than anything the world offers.

Take courage and conquer fear. Go God's way, not the way most of the world is going. If you stick with it, you will never regret it.

MARCH 17TH

Something to enjoy

Length of days is in her right hand. In her left hand are riches and honour.
(Proverbs 3:16)

We continue to look at the wonderful benefits for the person who has found God's wisdom and seeks to live by it. In this psalm, wisdom is personified as feminine, so this verse says that length of life is in wisdom's hand. What a statement! Live God's way and you will live longer; you will prosper and receive honour. Even if these things don't come your way in this life, you can be sure they will in the next. In heaven you will be living in a mansion and walking along streets paved with gold. God promises He will honour those who honour Him. Put away fear of what others may think or say and determine to seek God's way.

MARCH 18TH

Something more to enjoy

Her ways are ways of pleasantness.
(Proverbs 3:17)

The way of following God's wisdom is pleasantness. When life is pleasant there is no fear. Go with God.

MARCH 19TH

Something more to enjoy

All her paths are peace.
(Proverbs 3:17)

And even better than pleasantness is peace. Living God's way may not bring peace with everyone else, but you will know that you are at peace with God and what more could we ask for? When Jesus took all our punishment on the Cross, He bought our peace with God. We are free to enjoy God's love and blessing and know His power in our lives without any fear of His anger or displeasure. Thank You Jesus.

MARCH 20TH

Something more to enjoy

She is a tree of life to those who lay hold of her. Happy is everyone who retains her.
(Proverbs 3:18)

We finish these verses with a picture of God's wisdom as a tree of life which is available to you. Lay hold of her and keep hold of her and you will know true, lasting happiness. Fear will then have no place in your life.

MARCH 21ST

Something to put into practice

But if any of you lacks wisdom, let him ask of God, who gives to all liberally and without reproach, and it will be given to him. [6] But let him ask in faith, without any doubting, for he who doubts is like a wave of the sea, driven by the wind and tossed. [7] For that man shouldn't think that he will receive anything from the Lord. [8] He is a double-minded man, unstable in all his ways.
(James 1:5-8)

God's wisdom is always available to us but how do we take hold of it? First, know that when you ask God for wisdom, He doesn't assess whether you deserve it or not. He wants to give you wisdom simply because He loves you and longs for you to make the right choices in your life for your benefit. What a loving, generous God we have!

But God does put conditions on this promise. We have to ask in faith believing that He will answer, and not doubt. Do you ask God for wisdom and then keep on tossing the problem around in your mind? It's very easy to do that, but these verses say you are double-minded if you do it. Part of your mind has asked God and is waiting for His answer and the other part is still trying to work it out yourself. If you carry on like that God won't give you His wisdom.

Now this isn't easy, I know. But that doesn't mean we don't try. I've used these verses to discipline my thoughts quite a lot. I'm not saying I'm perfect at it, but I do know it's easier now than it used to be. Ask in faith and determine to wait in faith, casting anxious thoughts and doubt away. He will answer – God is faithful to all His promises.

MARCH 22ND

Something to act upon

David said to Solomon his son, "Be strong and courageous, and do it. Don't be afraid, nor be dismayed, for the LORD God, even my God, is with you. He will not fail you nor forsake you, until all the work for the service of the LORD's house is finished."

(1 Chronicles 28:20)

God had given the job of building His temple to David's son, Solomon. David encouraged Solomon to do the work and keep at it until it was done. He uses those same words we've heard quite a few times before – "Be strong and courageous." Building the temple was a huge job which would take many years. Solomon might have tired of it or given up, but he could remember his father's words and determined to see it through.

Maybe you are facing something big that God is calling you to do. Refuse to entertain fear of failure. Instead, remind yourself of your Father's words to be strong and courageous till the work is finished.

MARCH 23RD

Something to encourage you

"Most certainly, I tell you, one who doesn't enter by the door into the sheep fold, but climbs up some other way, is a thief and a robber. [2] But one who enters in by the door is the shepherd of the sheep. [3] The gatekeeper opens the gate for him, and the sheep listen to his voice. He calls his own sheep by name and leads them out."

(John 10:1-3)

Today we start to look at one of my favourite passages in the Bible – John 10:1-30. I'm going to pick out a few verses. In this passage Jesus is talking about His sheep – and you're one of them if you have accepted Jesus as your Lord and Saviour. Jesus is the only true shepherd of God's sheep.

In Jesus's day a shepherd would have looked after his sheep 24/7, living out in the fields with them, finding them good food and safe shelter and protecting them from harm. It wasn't just the flock that was important – each individual lamb and sheep was important too.

And Jesus says He is like the shepherd, caring for each one of us individually and leading us in the way He knows is best for us. If we know we have a perfect Shepherd looking after us, then why would we fear?

MARCH 24TH

Something to know

"Whenever he brings out his own sheep, he goes before them; and the sheep follow him, for they know his voice."
(John 10:4)

We will follow Jesus because we know His voice. That's what Jesus says. Have you ever wondered whether what you're hearing is from God or not? Don't agonise over it and get into fear about it. Instead, declare that you do know God's voice because Jesus says you do and wait for God's peace to show you what are His words and what are coming from somewhere else.

MARCH 25TH

Something to grasp

"My sheep hear my voice, and I know them, and they follow me."

(John 10:27)

Some verses later, Jesus says that His sheep hear His voice. Many times I've heard Christians say that they can't hear from God. Well, if they are truly born-again that just isn't true. Jesus says we do hear. So what's happening when we think we don't or can't? We're just not recognising His voice or we're not understanding it or we're drowning it out with all the stuff of life or maybe with fear.

When you're living with fear, it tends to take over and fill all your thoughts. You will hear God but you aren't able to take on board what He is saying. Your mind is too full. Thank God that you hear Him and ask Him to help you register what He is saying. Take time to get into His Word because that is the main way in which He speaks to you. Take comfort and don't be persuaded otherwise – you can hear God's voice and you can follow where He is leading – Jesus says so.

MARCH 26TH

Something to think about

"I give eternal life to them. They will never perish, and no one will snatch them out of my hand."

(John 10:28)

A shepherd can give the best life possible to His sheep, but Jesus gives eternal life. The Bible says eternal life is living in relationship with God which is for this life and for eternity when this life is over. There is no better life. Think on this when fear tries to fill you – you are living eternal life right now and forever. Hallelujah!

MARCH 27TH

Something to reassure you

"My Father who has given them to me is greater than all. No one is able to snatch them out of my Father's hand. [30] I and the Father are one."
(John 10:29-30)

These are the last two verses we are looking at from John 10. God is greater than anyone or anything in this world, however powerful and fearful they may seem. And you are held in His hand. Choose to believe this in faith and you will come to know it is true. And there's even more good news – no-one, yes no-one, can snatch you out of His hand. Don't be afraid – you are held safe in the hand of Almighty God.

MARCH 28TH

Something to decide on

When he had finished speaking, he said to Simon, "Put out into the deep and let down your nets for a catch." [5] Simon answered him, "Master, we worked all night and caught nothing; but at your word I will let down the net." [6] When they had done this, they caught a great multitude of fish, and their net was breaking. [7] They beckoned to their partners in the other boat, that they should come and help them. They came and filled both boats, so that they began to sink. [8] But Simon Peter, when he saw it, fell down at Jesus' knees, saying, "Depart from me, for I am a sinful man, Lord." [9] For he was amazed, and all who were with him, at the catch of fish which they had caught; [10] and so also were James and John, sons of Zebedee, who were partners with Simon. Jesus said to Simon, "Don't be afraid. From now on you will be catching people alive." [11] When they had brought their boats to land, they left everything, and followed him.

(Luke 5:4-11)

We all need to do what Jesus calls us to do. Don't just keep to the same routine for the sake of it however safe that might seem. There are amazing days ahead with Jesus – He can do the miraculous in your life.

Stepping out can seem frightening but with Jesus telling us not to fear and showing us the way to go, we really can step out with confidence in Him.

MARCH 29TH

Something to obey

"Be still, and know that I am God."
(Psalm 46:10)

Life is so busy but it's important to give ourselves time and space to know God. He tells us to be still. It is always good to stop physically in order to take time to concentrate on God and get to know Him better. But sometimes the activity we need to still, isn't so much in what we're doing, but in what's going on in our heads. If your mind is full of fear and worry you will find it hard to focus on your relationship with God. Still anxious thoughts and turn your mind to Jesus and you will find you are better able to get to know Him.

MARCH 30TH

Something to remember

My son, don't forget my teaching, but let your heart keep my commandments, [2] for they will add to you length of days, years of life, and peace.
(Proverbs 3:1-2)

Here is another reminder for us to remember God's Word and seek to live by it. If you are struggling with fear – get into God's Word and find for yourself how much He loves you and all His promises for you. They are what will give you peace. Fear and peace cannot live in the same place – choose peace through the Word of God.

MARCH 31ST

Something to take hold of

"When he, the Spirit of truth, has come, he will guide you into all truth."
(John 16:13)

After Jesus had died and rose again, He sent His Holy Spirit to live in all true believers and it is in this way that Jesus is always with us. Jesus told His disciples that His Holy Spirit would guide them into all truth. If you are confused and fearful about something, ask the Holy Spirit to guide you into the truth about what is going on. Ask in faith and He will show you.

April 1st

Something to do

"I have told you these things, that in me you may have peace. In the world you have trouble; but cheer up! I have overcome the world."

(John 16:33)

Jesus said these words to His disciples the day before He was going to be crucified. They were going to see the One they had followed and believed in and who had done so many amazing miracles, put to death. Their whole world was going to be rocked and they were going to feel abandoned and very afraid. And Jesus said, "Cheer up!"

But these weren't glib words. They were powerful words, because Jesus had overcome all the troubles of the world – big and small. On the Cross He would defeat the devil and everything he can try to throw at us. The disciples didn't understand this yet, but they would.

We live on this side of Jesus's death and resurrection – we live in the days when the world with all its trouble has finally been overcome by Jesus. Don't be afraid – cheer up!

APRIL 2ND

Something to take hold of

To this end the Son of God was revealed: that he might destroy the works of the devil.

(1 John 3:8)

This is why Jesus lived and died and came back to life – to defeat the devil and all his schemes. We have a mighty conqueror in Jesus who has already won the victory. With Him we're not on the winning side, we're on the side that has already won. Remember that when everything seems against you. Turn away from fear and towards Jesus, who has already won the victory so you can step into it.

APRIL 3RD

Something to understand

He himself bore our sins in his body on the tree, that we, having died to sins, might live to righteousness.
(1 Peter 2:24)

Jesus was the only perfect person who has ever lived or will ever live. He never sinned once. But as He hung on the Cross, God put all sin on Him – all the sin you and I have ever committed and the sin of everyone who has ever lived, is living and will live. He then suffered God's punishment for it all so we could be forgiven and made righteous – right with God. He suffered what He didn't deserve so we could have what we don't deserve – righteousness!

Don't be anxious and fearful about what you've done that you know is wrong. It's already been punished and all you have to do is receive the forgiveness Jesus has won for you. As a child of God, you are now forgiven and right with God. Wow! Thank You Jesus!

April 4th

Something more to understand

You were healed by his wounds.
(1 Peter 2:24)

Not only were your sins forgiven by Jesus's death, but your sicknesses and diseases were healed too. As Jesus suffered torture, He carried every single sickness and disease so we wouldn't have to. You are already healed in the spiritual realm – the job is done. It is now up to us to command sickness to go in the name of Jesus and receive our healing in faith. It really is that simple, but I know we can make it so difficult. Everything around us and things said to us and our own thoughts will try to tell us we are sick. We can see or feel the physical evidence. It is so easy to be afraid when we are sick. But God is greater than what our five senses tell us.

Go with the truth of the healing Jesus has won for you and persevere. Nothing can change what He has done for you. Step away from fear and into your healing today.

APRIL 5TH

Something to reassure you

Now after the Sabbath, as it began to dawn on the first day of the week, Mary Magdalene and the other Mary came to see the tomb. [2] Behold, there was a great earthquake, for an angel of the Lord descended from the sky and came and rolled away the stone from the door and sat on it. [3] His appearance was like lightning, and his clothing white as snow. [4] For fear of him, the guards shook, and became like dead men. [5] The angel answered the women, "Don't be afraid, for I know that you seek Jesus, who has been crucified. [6] He is not here, for he has risen, just like he said. Come, see the place where the Lord was lying.

(Matthew 28:1-6)

When the women went to Jesus's tomb on the first Easter morning, they found the stone which sealed it rolled away and His body wasn't there. Their response was to be afraid. Then an angel reassured them that He had risen from the dead just as He had said He would.

When you're tempted to fear, reassure yourself that Jesus has risen from the dead, having defeated everything that would try to make you afraid. He loves you, is on your side and will never, ever leave you. Good news indeed!

APRIL 6TH

Something to determine

"Go quickly and tell his disciples, 'He has risen from the dead, and behold, he goes before you into Galilee; there you will see him.' Behold, I have told you."
(Matthew 28:7)

The angel then told the women to go quickly and tell Jesus's disciples that He had risen and that He will see them in Galilee. He finishes with the words, "Behold, I have told you." When you know clearly that God has spoken to you through His Word or in your spirit, believe it. Don't allow your minds to get into turmoil about it. Behold, He has spoken.

APRIL 7TH

Something to rejoice about

As they went to tell his disciples, behold, Jesus met them, saying, "Rejoice!" They came and took hold of his feet, and worshipped him. [10] Then Jesus said to them, "Don't be afraid. Go tell my brothers that they should go into Galilee, and there they will see me."

(Matthew 28:9-10)

What joy for these women to meet with the risen Jesus. I can imagine them feeling fear as well as joy as they realised who He was and what had happened. They were the first witnesses of the most momentous event in history.

Don't let fear stop you from experiencing the love and joy of Jesus. Hear Him say to you, "Don't be afraid." Respond to Him with worship and seek to follow in the way He directs you. It is the way of peace.

APRIL 8TH

Something to act upon

When they had laid many stripes on them, they threw them into prison, charging the jailer to keep them safely. [24] Having received such a command, he threw them into the inner prison and secured their feet in the stocks. [25] But about midnight Paul and Silas were praying and singing hymns to God, and the prisoners were listening to them.
(Acts 16:23-25)

After Jesus had sent the Holy Spirit to live in the disciples with power, they went straight out and started telling people about Him. The religious leaders thought they had put an end to Jesus and His teaching when they crucified Him, but now His followers had greatly increased and were teaching others about Him, everywhere they went.

When Saul, a devout pharisee, was converted, his name was changed to Paul and he set out to tell many people around the known world about Jesus, giving them the good news of salvation in Him. Eventually the religious leaders arrested him and Silas, beat them, and threw them into prison. Not only were they locked up, but their feet were held in stocks. How did Paul and Silas react? Did they let fear get hold of them? Did they talk about what might happen and what their chances of escaping death were? No – they prayed and sang hymns to God. What an example.

We may never have to face prison for our faith in Jesus, but we all face difficult situations where the outlook doesn't look good. Let's follow Paul and Silas's example and sing praises to God instead of allowing fear to grow. The great thing is that when we truly praise God, fear disappears.

APRIL 9TH

Something to remember

Suddenly there was a great earthquake, so that the foundations of the prison were shaken; and immediately all the doors were opened, and everyone's bonds were loosened. 27 The jailer, being roused out of sleep and seeing the prison doors open, drew his sword and was about to kill himself, supposing that the prisoners had escaped.
28 But Paul cried with a loud voice, saying, "Don't harm yourself, for we are all here!" 29 He called for lights, sprang in, fell down trembling before Paul and Silas, 30 brought them out, and said, "Sirs, what must I do to be saved?"
(Acts 16:26-30)

So what happened next? God sent an earthquake to open the doors of the prison and loosen the bonds holding all of the prisoners. When the jailer realised what had happened, he was about to kill himself because he presumed all the prisoners had fled. But Paul called to him and told him they were all still there. Not only had Paul and Silas not made a break for it, but neither had all the other prisoners. The end result was the jailer coming to faith in Jesus.

When we refuse to fear and choose to praise God instead, even when we don't feel like it, then amazing things can happen.

APRIL 10TH

Something to take hold of

Be strong, all you people of the land,' says the LORD, 'and work, for I am with you,' says the LORD of Armies. [5] This is the word that I covenanted with you when you came out of Egypt, and my Spirit lived amongst you. 'Don't be afraid.'

(Haggai 2:4-5)

When God's people returned to Jerusalem from exile in Babylon, they found that the temple had been destroyed. They set about rebuilding it, but it was such a huge task that they soon got tired of it and concentrated on getting their own houses and lands and businesses in order instead.

The prophet Haggai kept encouraging the people and their leaders to go back to the work of rebuilding the temple. God spoke through him, telling them not to be afraid, but to get on with the work. He told them to be strong. Obviously physical strength would be needed, but I believe God was telling them to be strong in their thinking as well. It's easy to look at a big task ahead of you and feel weak and afraid. Will I be able to do it? Will I last the course? Will I fail? What will others think if I do?

God reminded them how He had supernaturally helped their ancestors when He brought them out of Egypt and reassured them that His Word stood today just as powerfully as it did then.

Are you facing something big which you know you should be doing? Don't be afraid. God will help you. His Word is as powerful today as it ever has been and it is as powerful for you as it is for anyone else who will take hold of it.

April 11th

Something to act upon

Praise the LORD, my soul! All that is within me, praise his holy name!

(Psalm 103:1)

Today we start looking at the first five verses of my favourite psalm – Psalm 103. It starts with the writer telling himself to praise God. Sometimes this is what we need to do. We don't always feel like praising, in fact we may feel worried or downcast. But we know praise will lift us up and help us, so it's time to tell ourselves to just do it. And not half-heartedly while we still think about our problems, but with everything that is in us. Go for it and it will help. You will see.

April 12th

Something to remember

Praise the LORD, my soul, and don't forget all his benefits …

(Psalm 103:2)

And as you praise God, think about all Jesus has done and won for you. The psalmist was writing before the time of Jesus, but remember, all the promises of the Old Testament are 'Yes' in Jesus. He has made them all available to you through His death and resurrection. The more you think of all you have because of Jesus, the more you will want to praise Him – it's an upward spiral which will banish fear.

APRIL 13TH

Something to take on board

... who forgives all your sins ...
(Psalm 103:3)

Now begins a list of five benefits that God has won for you through Jesus.

Firstly, He has forgiven all your sins – not just some, but ALL. That in itself deals with a lot of fear – fear of anger, of condemnation, of punishment. Praise God!

APRIL 14TH

Something to rejoice about

... who heals all your diseases ...
(Psalm 103:3)

Secondly, he has healed all your diseases. Again, not some of them but ALL – even the ones the doctors can't cure. What a lot of time we can spend worrying about our health. Here's the answer to all those fears – Jesus.

APRIL 15TH

Something to grasp

… who redeems your life from destruction …
(Psalm 103:4)

Thirdly, He redeems our lives from destruction. Without Jesus you are on your way to hell. Yes, it does exist. However, God doesn't want you to go there – He wants you in heaven with Him; but if you reject Jesus there is only one place to go when you die. Don't be fooled – the destruction isn't something that is done and then it's over. It is living forever in a place of destruction without it ever ending. No-one would want to spend a moment there, never mind eternity.

But praise God, you don't have to. Accept Jesus as your Lord and Saviour and He will save you from hell and you will live with Him in everlasting joy and peace. The answer to a fear of hell is to turn to Jesus and be born-again.

April 16th

Something to build you up

... who crowns you with loving kindness and tender mercies ...

(Psalm 103:4)

Fourthly, God crowns you with loving kindness and tender mercies. You are given a crown to honour you. God wants to honour you for your faithfulness to Him. And what a crown – God's love and kindness on your head and flowing over you along with His mercy which was won for you by Jesus on the Cross. Know that God's love for you is kind and tender.

Think on that when fear tries to come. In your imagination see yourself crowned by God with love and mercy. Fear will have to go as you are built up in all Jesus has done and won for you. Thank You Lord!

APRIL 17TH

Something to enjoy

… who satisfies your desire with good things …
(Psalm 103:5)

And lastly, God satisfies your desire with good things. When we are in a love relationship with God, we will want the things which God wants and He will satisfy those desires. And they will always be good. In those times when you don't feel God's love, remember it is still true and strong and kind and tender.

Don't let fear rob you of the truth. Praise Him and thank Him for all the things He has given you and has for you. Remember all His benefits.

April 18th

Something to lift your heart

... so that your youth is renewed like the eagle's.
(Psalm 103:5)

And the result? Your youth will be renewed – your strength, your energy, your alertness, your health etc. Praise God! "Fear, look at all Jesus has done for me. You have to go in His name."

APRIL 19TH

Something to remember

"Don't be afraid of them, for there is nothing covered that will not be revealed, or hidden that will not be known."
(Matthew 10:26)

When wrong things are said about you or done to you, determine not to be afraid of the people who have said or done them. Remember that one day everything will come to light and the truth of the matter will be revealed. If it doesn't happen in this life, it will certainly happen in the next. Jesus said so – trust Him. He is faithful.

APRIL 20TH

Something to rejoice about

... giving thanks to the Father, who made us fit to be partakers of the inheritance of the saints in light, [13] who delivered us out of the power of darkness, and translated us into the Kingdom of the Son of his love, [14] in whom we have our redemption, the forgiveness of our sins.
(Colossians 1:12-14)

When we were born-again, God instantly took us out of the kingdom of darkness which is ruled by the devil, and into the Kingdom of light ruled by Jesus. It's not because we deserve it or have earned it. It's because Jesus has won our forgiveness and made us righteous – right with God. It's all God's doing, not ours.

Thank Him and praise Him. You are forgiven, living in the light of Jesus – that's enough to silence fear. Make it your focus and rejoice in it.

APRIL 21ST

Something to take on board

"Everyone therefore who hears these words of mine and does them, I will liken him to a wise man who built his house on a rock. [25] The rain came down, the floods came, and the winds blew and beat on that house; and it didn't fall, for it was founded on the rock. [26] Everyone who hears these words of mine and doesn't do them will be like a foolish man who built his house on the sand. [27] The rain came down, the floods came, and the winds blew and beat on that house; and it fell—and its fall was great."
(Matthew 7:24-27)

This is Jesus speaking. He is painting a picture of two different people who base their lives on two different things. The first person built his life on God's Word. He made it the basis for all his thoughts, words, decisions and actions. When trouble came along, he was able to come through and out the other side with his life intact. The second man based his life on his own ideas and what the world said about things. When trouble came, he found he had nothing true to help him and his life fell apart dramatically.

It's a powerful picture. Take it on board and decide to build your life on the truth of God's Word alone. Then you will not need to fear when the storm hits. You will know that you have a solid foundation in Jesus to take you through and safely out the other side.

APRIL 22ND

Something to understand

But he who is joined to the Lord is one spirit.
(1 Corinthians 6:17)

Just one sentence today, but what a sentence! When you are born-again you are joined to Jesus as one spirit. Remember, God gives you a brand-new spirit when you are saved and also Jesus comes to live in you by His Holy Spirit. The Holy Spirit lives in your perfect spirit and they mesh together as one. Wow! You and Jesus are one! How can fear remain in you in the face of that truth!

April 23rd

Something to encourage you

"Blessed are you when people reproach you, persecute you, and say all kinds of evil against you falsely, for my sake. [12] Rejoice, and be exceedingly glad, for great is your reward in heaven. For that is how they persecuted the prophets who were before you."
(Matthew 5:11-12)

Today I want to remind you that, as a believer, you will face persecution for your faith in some way. But Jesus tells us to rejoice when it happens. Our natural reaction to persecution is to be angry or fearful, so it takes a determination to turn away from those emotions and rejoice. Jesus encourages us by telling us that there will be a reward in heaven for us and also that we're not the only ones who have suffered persecution. It's happened since the first believers were baptised in the Holy Spirit.

If persecution comes your way, say out loud, "I refuse to fear. I choose to rejoice in Jesus my Saviour," and then start thanking Him and praising Him for His love and faithfulness.

APRIL 24TH

Something to think about

Therefore I take pleasure in weaknesses, in injuries, in necessities, in persecutions, and in distresses, for Christ's sake. For when I am weak, then am I strong.
(2 Corinthians 12:10)

Paul says he takes pleasure in things done to him because of his faith. Why would he do that? Because he knows that though he is weak, God is in Him and God is strong. He knows that He will help him through. Don't be fearful. Realise that God is strong in you and enough for anything that you face.

April 25th

<u>Something to take hold of</u>

God, who gives life to the dead, and calls the things that are not, as though they were.
(Romans 4:17)

God calls things that are not, as though they were. When this verse first registered with me it was a revelation. Sometimes you may feel you haven't got any faith, but the truth is you have. What's happening is that unbelief is affecting it. Jesus said that you only need faith the size of a mustard seed as long as there is no doubt or unbelief alongside it. God looks at things with faith, not physical eyesight and He wants us to do the same.

When God sees someone sick, He sees them well because He has already won their healing for them on the Cross. When Jesus saw Jairus's dead daughter, He said she was asleep because He knew she was going to come back to life.

In the example which follows this verse, God had promised Abraham that He would be the father of nations, yet he and his wife had no children, and Sarah was now beyond child-bearing age. But Abraham believed what God said. He called things that were not (childlessness) as though they were – father of many nations. He held onto his faith until he saw it come to pass. He had a son called Isaac and his descendants became the Jewish nation.

When things go contrary to God's will in your life, take hold of your faith; knock unbelief and fear on the head with the truth of God's Word and wait in certain hope. Refuse to speak doubt and fear. Call things that are not as though they were and they will become reality.

APRIL 26TH

Something to declare

"Don't be afraid, for I have redeemed you. I have called you by your name. You are mine."
(Isaiah 43:1)

When Jesus suffered your punishment in your place, He paid the price for your sin. So, when you accept Him you are then redeemed. God has bought you back. He loves you unconditionally and individually. Each one of us is uniquely special to Him. He has called each one of us by name.

You are His – believe it and declare it in the face of fear. Say, "I am not afraid, for God has redeemed me. He has called me by my name. I am His. Thank You Lord!"

April 27th

Something to reassure you

Then he said to me, "Don't be afraid, Daniel; for from the first day that you set your heart to understand, and to humble yourself before your God, your words were heard. I have come for your words' sake. [13] But the prince of the kingdom of Persia withstood me twenty-one days; but, behold, Michael, one of the chief princes, came to help me because I remained there with the kings of Persia."
(Daniel 10:12-13)

Daniel had prayed to God on other occasions and seen his prayers answered immediately, but this time the answer didn't come for three weeks. Daniel had started to fear. Maybe he thought that God hadn't heard him or didn't want to answer him. Then an angel came to Daniel and explained that God had indeed heard his prayer and that he had now come with the answer. The reason he was delayed wasn't because God didn't answer straightaway, but because the devil had tried his best to stop the answer reaching Daniel. There was a spiritual battle going on, but God's angel won through and brought Daniel his answer.

If you feel fearful if your prayers don't seem to be answered, remember Daniel and the angel. God always hears and answers prayers that are prayed according to His will. Be reassured.

April 28th

Something to act upon

Now therefore let your hands be strong, and be valiant.
(2 Samuel 2:7)

We've already seen that fear can paralyse us, until it's hard to do anything. Here God tells us to just get on and do what we are supposed to do. Don't sit round being idle – fear can really take hold when you do nothing. It's much better to get stuck into something. It may take courage to get going but remember, God is with you and encouraging you and helping you and that makes all the difference. You're not trying to do things in your own strength, but in the strength of the Lord and that silences fear.

April 29th

Something to do

Why are you in despair, my soul? Why are you disturbed within me? Hope in God! For I shall still praise him, the saving help of my countenance, and my God.
(Psalm 42:11)

Do you ever feel in despair? Are your thoughts and emotions ever disturbed? I would think all of us have felt that at some time in our lives and for some it may be a frequent experience. It's a horrible feeling. So how do we get out of it, turn away from fear and start to feel positive again? This psalm gives us the answer. Praise God. Yes, even when you don't want to, even when everything in you says there's no point. Just do it and you will find that He will help you. He is your Saviour and your God – to who else could you turn!

April 30th

Something to stand on

Moses said to the people, "Don't be afraid. Stand still, and see the salvation of the LORD, which he will work for you today; for you will never again see the Egyptians whom you have seen today. [14] The LORD will fight for you, and you shall be still."
(Exodus 14:13-14)

Moses had led the Israelites out of slavery in Egypt. They had come to the shore of the Red Sea and the Egyptians were following behind to capture them. The people were afraid and no doubt started to panic. Moses spoke to them, turning their thoughts to the Lord. He told them not to fear but to stand still and see what God was going to do to save them. Their job was to be still. I'm sure that, as well as literally standing still and not panicking, God was also telling them to still their anxious thoughts.

So what happened? Moses did what God told him to do – he held his rod out over the sea and the waters divided making a dry path for the Israelites to walk across to the other side! They walked safely across and when the Egyptians tried to follow them, God told Moses to stretch his rod out again. The waters closed across and all their enemies were drowned; they never saw them again just as Moses had said. They certainly saw the salvation of the Lord that day.

When you seem to be in a no-win situation that is making you afraid, stand still, and see the salvation of the LORD, which He wants to work for you today, The LORD will fight for you, and you shall be still.

MAY 1ST

Something to encourage you

For you will light my lamp, LORD. My God will light up my darkness. [29] For by you, I advance through a troop. By my God, I leap over a wall.

(Psalm 18:28-29)

God is the light of the world. Only He can light up your darkness. We all know how frightening darkness can seem. Do you remember as a child wanting the light left on at night or your bedroom door open so the light from outside could come in? Even as an adult, walking along a dark road can seem a bit scary.

If you find yourself having dark thoughts, don't spend your time trying to get rid of the darkness. You will never be able to shovel it out. Darkness is simply the absence of light. So instead, turn the light on and the darkness is gone. Switch the light of God on – turn your thoughts to Him and His truth. Then His light will shine to show you the way through and out of the situations that make you fearful. With His light leading you, you can do amazing things for God.

MAY 2ND

Something to stand on

I will pursue my enemies, and overtake them. I won't turn away until they are consumed. [38] I will strike them through, so that they will not be able to rise. They shall fall under my feet. [39] For you have armed me with strength to the battle. You have subdued under me those who rose up against me.

(Psalm 18:37-39)

Our battle as born-again Christians is not against people, but against the devil. He may use other people to attack us, but our fight is with him.

So how can we fight him? God has armed you with strength for the battle. He has put a sword in your hand – the perfect weapon to strike the devil through. Ephesians 6:17 tells us it is 'the sword of the Spirit, which is the word of God.' And Hebrews 4:12 says that – 'the word of God is living and active, and sharper than any two-edged sword, piercing even to the dividing of soul and spirit, of both joints and marrow, and is able to discern the thoughts and intentions of the heart.' God's Word is more powerful than any physical sword. It will enable you to distinguish right from wrong and to discern where thoughts and words are coming from.

When the devil starts to whisper his accusations, lies, doubt and fear in your ear or through other people, strike him through with the Word of God. You already have lots of declarations to use in this book. Be persistent. Don't give up. Use your sword each day and the devil will fall under your feet.

MAY 3RD

Something to act upon

Hear the word which the LORD speaks to you, house of Israel! [2] The LORD says, "Don't learn the way of the nations, and don't be dismayed at the signs of the sky; for the nations are dismayed at them."

(Jeremiah 10:1-2)

These are such important words from God to His people. Don't let yourself be influenced by the way the world looks at things and by the conclusions they draw. The media loves to present gloom and doom and discuss worst possible scenarios which people pick up on and take as truth. The end result is dismay in their minds and their hearts.

We are living through the COVID 19 pandemic as I write and it is obvious that so much of the fear around is generated by the way the media reports on it.

Don't learn the ways of the world. Be wise about what you watch and listen to. Guard your mind and heart from negativity and fear and you will not be dismayed as others are.

MAY 4TH

Something to realise

Blessed be the God and Father of our Lord Jesus Christ, who has blessed us with every spiritual blessing in the heavenly places in Christ.
(Ephesians 1:3)

Here is another of my favourite verses. Paul is talking to believers. He says that God has already blessed us with every blessing. Remember, every promise which God had made to His people in the Old Testament was stamped 'Yes' by Jesus and every promise made since then is ours through Him too. Every possible blessing is already ours because it has been won for us by Jesus in the spiritual realm.

Do you experience all the blessings of God? If not, it's not because they aren't yours. They already have your name on them. You just need to believe in them and take hold of them. Don't blame God when things are difficult and fear starts to creep in. Go to His Word; find His promises and receive them, giving thanks and praise to God. The more you do it, the more you will experience all God's blessings. He is good and faithful.

May 5th

Something to obey

"You will hear of wars and rumours of wars. See that you aren't troubled, for all this must happen, but the end is not yet."

(Matthew 24:6)

We know that the world is full of war and conflict and has been ever since man first sinned. It's so easy to worry and become fearful of what is happening and what might happen to us and to those we love. But this is Jesus speaking and He says, "See that you aren't troubled." That's a command, so it must be possible. Don't let your emotions run away with you. Counter them with the unchanging truth of God's Word and defeat fear.

MAY 6TH

Something to declare

My God will supply every need of yours according to his riches in glory in Christ Jesus.
(Philippians 4:19)

This is another of my favourite verses – it's inevitable that a lot of them have got into this book! The question is – do we really believe this? Or is it just something nice to read and then we forget all about it when things get difficult. Whenever we fear, we are actually not believing these words of God. That's quite challenging for you and for me.

Speak these words out loud until they become a part of you. Remember, faith comes by hearing and hearing by the Word of God. Build yourself up in this truth now, so that when you need to depend on it, a foundation of faith is already laid. I heard someone say that you prepare for battle in times of peace. It's no good waiting until you need to believe this and hoping that it will somehow work. You need to set this promise firmly in your mind and your heart so its truth is ready for you when you need it.

God is a God of bounty. He longs to pour His blessings and provision into your life till you're overflowing. Note it is EVERY need that He will supply, not just some. And note that He WILL supply every need. The supply is there, but we have to take hold of it in faith. When you lack anything, be it something physical or God's wisdom, ask Him and thank Him for it before you see it. He will supply it. He is faithful to His Word.

MAY 7TH

Something to stand on

"When you go out to battle against your enemies, and see horses, chariots, and a people more numerous than you, you shall not be afraid of them; for the LORD your God, who brought you up out of the land of Egypt, is with you."
(Deuteronomy 20:1)

We all face battles in our lives and some of them can make us quite fearful if we're not careful. When we know we are taking a stand for God and His truth, we can be sure that He is with us. If God Almighty is on our side, how can we possibly lose! Turn away from fear and put your trust in the Lord your God. Remember, you are on the side that has already won!

MAY 8TH

Something to take hold of

The LORD will give strength to his people. The LORD will bless his people with peace.

(Psalm 29:11)

What a lovely promise. Do you feel weak and are your thoughts more fearful than peaceful? Take hold of this promise; speak it out loud. Allow it to build your faith up and silence fear. Go forward in faith, expecting to see it come to pass.

May 9th

Something to reassure you

The LORD, your God, is amongst you, a mighty one who will save. He will rejoice over you with joy. He will calm you in his love. He will rejoice over you with singing.
(Zephaniah 3:17)

Here's another of my favourite verses. What a wonderful picture. God Himself is amongst us – He is actually within each one of us who have given our life to Jesus. He takes such delight in us – each one of us individually. He expresses His joy in us by singing over us! And He seeks to calm our fears and anxious thoughts by assuring us of His love for us. Let this reassure you. Picture God singing over you and calming you with His love. Allow it to wash your fears away and simply enjoy His delight in you.

May 10th

Something to declare

But you are a chosen race, a royal priesthood, a holy nation, a people for God's own possession, that you may proclaim the excellence of him who called you out of darkness into his marvellous light.

(1 Peter 2:9)

God chose you. He didn't ordain for you to be saved and others not, but He has always known who would accept Jesus. He has made you royal – He crowns you with loving-kindness. You belong to His church – true believers who serve Him and seek to live a holy life. You belong to God. He called you out of the darkness of the world of the devil and into the marvellous light of Jesus. You are not destined for hell, but for glory in Heaven. Wow – what a list! And He has called us to tell others of Jesus and the way to salvation.

Make this a declaration. Change 'you' to 'I' or 'me'. Fear has no place when we truly believe this.

MAY 11TH

Something to know

For him who knew no sin he made to be sin on our behalf, so that in him we might become the righteousness of God.
(2 Corinthians 5:21)

The amazing truth is that God didn't only put all our sin on Jesus; Jesus actually became that sin. This is something difficult for us to get our heads round. Jesus took on our sin so profoundly that he actually became it, with all its weight and guilt and shame. We can all think of something we've done which can cause us to wake in the middle of the night with fear. Jesus became that one sin for me. Add to it all my other sins and all your sins and all the sins of the entire human race and He became it all. It is beyond imagination.

The suffering this caused Him would have been far greater than the horrendous physical suffering of the torture and death He went through. And He did it all so we could be forgiven and set free and become right with God – righteous, just as He is righteous. He became our sin so we could become His righteousness. What a Saviour! This is how much He loves us.

Next time fear strikes at something you have done in your past, refuse to entertain thoughts of shame, guilt and condemnation. Rejoice in your Saviour who has suffered so much so you can be free to go forward with Him, not chained to your past. Thank You Jesus.

MAY 12TH

Something to obey

"Only be strong and courageous."
(Joshua 1:18)

Remember Joshua leading the Israelites into the land God had promised them? God reminds him and us again to be strong and courageous. And He said to only be strong and courageous. Don't be fearful or dismayed, only strong and courageous. Remember, in your spirit you have the mind of Christ. Send fear packing and rejoice in God's strength and courage in you.

MAY 13TH

Something to grasp

For as the rain comes down and the snow from the sky, and doesn't return there, but waters the earth, and makes it grow and bud, and gives seed to the sower and bread to the eater; [11] so is my word that goes out of my mouth: it will not return to me void, but it will accomplish that which I please, and it will prosper in the thing I sent it to do.
(Isaiah 55:10-11)

God's Word is powerful. He created the whole universe by speaking it into being. When God speaks there is real purpose. And He will fulfil that purpose in our lives when we let Him. Just as surely as rain falls from the sky and enables our food to grow, God's Word will do what He intends it to do.

When He promises you something, it isn't empty words; it isn't a case of maybe He will or maybe He won't. It is power for you to take hold of and see fulfilled. Don't be afraid of appropriating God's Word for yourself. Believe it and receive it and see all that He will do.

MAY 14TH

<u>Something to understand</u>

They are of the world. Therefore they speak of the world, and the world hears them. [6] We are of God. He who knows God listens to us. He who is not of God doesn't listen to us. By this we know the spirit of truth, and the spirit of error.
(1 John 4:5-6)

How do you know whether what someone is saying is of God or of the world? If someone is of God, they will listen to us when we speak of His truth. If they are just worldly, they will readily listen to each other, but not to us. Don't be afraid of what the world says or of standing against it. Turn away from the spirit of error and take hold of the spirit of truth.

MAY 15TH

Something to put into practice

It is better to take refuge in the LORD, than to put confidence in man. [9] It is better to take refuge in the LORD, than to put confidence in princes.
(Psalm 118:8-9)

Man might appear to have the answers, especially those who are in the public eye, such as celebrities and leaders and 'experts'. But don't put your confidence in them unless what they say lines up with the truth of God. Put your confidence in the Lord instead and run to Him for safety when things get difficult and you feel fear welling up. He has the real answer and will never let you down.

MAY 16TH

Something to declare

I am still confident of this: I will see the goodness of the LORD in the land of the living.
(Psalm 27:13)

Whatever happens today, instead of entertaining fear, make this your declaration.

MAY 17TH

Something to be watchful for

Be sober and self-controlled. Be watchful. Your adversary, the devil, walks around like a roaring lion, seeking whom he may devour. [9] Withstand him steadfast in your faith, knowing that your brothers who are in the world are undergoing the same sufferings.

(1 Peter 5:8-9)

We need to be alert because, as followers of Jesus, we have an enemy. We can only be alert if we are in our right minds, so we are told to be sober and self-controlled. Our enemy is the devil. Does that strike fear in you straightaway? Well, read on.

The devil walks around like a roaring lion. That is LIKE a lion – he isn't a lion. He doesn't have that physical strength. He can only attack you in your thinking. It is when someone listens to his lies and takes them onboard that he can have an inroad into their life and can start to cause problems.

And notice that he is looking for who he may devour. That means he can't devour everyone. If you stay firm in your faith in Jesus, knowing what He has done for you and who you are in Him, then you can resist Him and you are undevourable.

So there is no need to fear. In fact, if you start to be afraid of the devil you are listening to his lies. Instead, rejoice in your Saviour, thanking Him and praising Him. Don't give the devil any space in your thinking, but do be alert so you quickly recognise any deception he tries to whisper in your ear. Then you can withstand him and he has to flee and take his fear with him.

MAY 18TH

Something to declare

God is our refuge and strength, a very present help in trouble. [2] Therefore we won't be afraid, though the earth changes, though the mountains are shaken into the heart of the seas; [3] though its waters roar and are troubled, though the mountains tremble with their swelling.

(Psalm 46:1-3)

We are living in such strange times. The whole world is changing as a result of COVID 19, and natural disasters are continuing to happen. The psalmist here tells himself that he will not be afraid whatever happens. He makes a determined decision. And he can do that because he knows His God – that He is always with him to help in times of trouble. He declares that God will strengthen him and protect him.

Let's make his declaration our declaration and speak it out in the face of fear. Declare your trust in God with boldness, and fear will be silenced. Hallelujah!

MAY 19TH

Something to act on

This is the day that the LORD has made. We will rejoice and be glad in it!
(Psalm 118:24)

You may have woken today with fear in your heart, but turn away from it by declaring this out loud. God loves you, He is on your side and He has an answer for everything that you will face today. Choose to be glad about that and rejoice in it.

MAY 20TH

Something to determine

"But watch yourselves, for they will deliver you up to councils. You will be beaten in synagogues. You will stand before rulers and kings for my sake, for a testimony to them. [10] The Good News must first be preached to all the nations. [11] When they lead you away and deliver you up, don't be anxious beforehand or premeditate what you will say, but say whatever will be given you in that hour. For it is not you who speak, but the Holy Spirit."

(Mark 13:9-11)

Some years ago, it was difficult to imagine we would ever be brought before courts in the UK because of our faith, but there have now been several cases where Christians have been accused because they acted in accordance with their faith.

None of us would want that to happen to us, but take note of what Jesus says in these verses. He tells us not to be anxious beforehand, worrying about what we should say in defence of our faith. Really? Yes, really – because it is Jesus who says it.

Let's determine now, before anything happens, that if it does, we will trust the Holy Spirit to give us the words to say. Thank You Holy Spirit.

MAY 21ST

Something to rejoice about

If you are insulted for the name of Christ, you are blessed, because the Spirit of glory and of God rests on you. On their part he is blasphemed, but on your part he is glorified.

(1 Peter 4:14)

This is a great verse to follow yesterday's. If we are persecuted because of Jesus, be it in a big or a small way, and we remain faithful no matter what, God is glorified and we are blessed by Him. Hallelujah! Read this and rejoice about it – the Spirit of glory (all the goodness of God shining in His perfect light) and God Himself rests on you. Wow! That should silence fear.

Use your imagination to see yourself blessed by God like this, not to puff yourself up, but to take your focus off fear and help you to rejoice in God your glorified Saviour.

MAY 22ND

Something to understand

His divine power has granted to us all things that pertain to life and godliness, through the knowledge of him who called us by his own glory and virtue, [4] by which he has granted to us his precious and exceedingly great promises; that through these you may become partakers of the divine nature, having escaped from the corruption that is in the world by lust.

(2 Peter 1:3-4)

Living without fear is possible, however difficult it may seem, because when you became a born-again Christian, God gave you everything you need to live His way, which is always the best way and has nothing to do with fear. We spend the rest of our lives learning from God's Word how to do it. Seek more and more of His truth to help you live your life day by day without fear.

May 23rd

Something to declare

Let the weak say, 'I am strong.'
(Joel 3:10)

Do you feel weak? Dwelling on your weakness is the way to anxiety. Dwelling on the power of God in you will silence fear. Remember God calling things that are not, as though they are? Jesus has overcome all our weaknesses so even if you feel weak, you can declare in Him, "I am strong." Praise God!

May 24th

Something to stand on

Hear, Israel, you draw near today to battle against your enemies. Don't let your heart faint! Don't be afraid, nor tremble, neither be scared of them; [4] for the LORD your God is he who goes with you, to fight for you against your enemies, to save you.

(Deuteronomy 20:3-4)

These are words Moses spoke to the Israelites as they prepared for battle. We may not be facing armed combat, but we all face battles in our lives. Some of them are of our own making, but many are the enemy attacking us because of our faith in Jesus. Don't shrink from the battle – don't be afraid or tremble or be scared of the devil. Jesus has already won the victory over him.

Be alert to what he is whispering in your ear and fight it knowing that God is with you and the devil is already a defeated foe. Stand with Jesus and His victory becomes yours.

May 25th

Something to put into practice

My son, attend to my words. Turn your ear to my sayings.
21 Let them not depart from your eyes. Keep them in the
centre of your heart. 22 For they are life to those who find
them, and health to their whole body.
(Proverbs 4:20-22)

God always calls us to get into His Word – to read it; think about what it says; let it settle right in the centre of our hearts. Do this sincerely, flowing out of your relationship with God, not as a ritual or a duty. Believe what God says and receive it and apply its truth to all you think, say and do.

The more you do this, the more of God's truth you will have in the centre of your heart to draw on when things go wrong. Fear may try to get in your mind, but you have the word of God to speak against it in faith and power. Remember, you prepare for battle in times of peace. Start to attend to God's words today and you will have power ready for anything. You will find that the truth of God's Word will truly give you life and physical health. Thank You Lord!

MAY 26TH

Something to determine

When I am afraid, I will put my trust in you. [4] In God, I praise his word. In God, I put my trust. I will not be afraid.
(Psalm 56:3-4)

The psalmist knew full well that fear can so easily come, so he made a decision before it came that He would put his trust in God. He would praise Him for His word. And because of this, he can say with confidence that he will not be afraid, no matter what.

A wonderful example for us to follow. It takes determination and perseverance but it is so worth it.

MAY 27TH

<u>God's Word</u>

Your word is a lamp to my feet, and a light for my path.
(Psalm 119:105)

God's Word is the best guide we have. It will show us where to put our next step as it lights our feet, and it will shine forwards on the path so we can see the way ahead.

God doesn't usually show us all the details of the journey as we step out with Him – He leads us a step or a few steps at a time. But it is His Word which will help us along the way, showing us if we are on course or veering off. If you are stepping out for God, don't be afraid of what might be ahead; let God's Word guide you and He will get you there.

MAY 28TH

<u>Something to remember</u>

Then they cry to the LORD in their trouble, and he brings them out of their distress. [29] He makes the storm a calm, so that its waves are still. [30] Then they are glad because it is calm, so he brings them to their desired haven.

(Psalm 107:28-30)

When trouble hits, turn to God straightaway, knowing He is able to help you and will bring you through. God has a plan for your life and He will do all He can to bring it to pass, but He won't bypass your free will. Don't fear when problems arise, call out to God, put your trust in Him and stand on His Word and see His plan unfold.

MAY 29TH

Something to know

Don't you know that your body is a temple of the Holy Spirit who is in you, whom you have from God?
(1 Corinthians 6:19)

If you are born-again, then it is a fact that God's Holy Spirit lives in you. In the days before Jesus, God dwelt among His people in the temple in Jerusalem. But after Jesus had ascended back into heaven, He sent the Holy Spirit to live in His believers. Now your body is the temple of the Holy Spirit. Don't doubt it for a second, even when you can't feel His presence. Don't let fear tell you it isn't true. Know it as fact whatever happens – it is indeed the truth of God.

May 30th

Something to reassure

The Spirit himself testifies with our spirit that we are children of God.

(Romans 8:16)

I have found that a lot of Christians can doubt if they are really saved. It's a tactic the devil will use against us and it can bring real fear with it. Remember, God's Holy Spirit lives in our born-again spirit and they are united as one. And His Holy Spirit reassures our spirit that we are indeed His children and on our way to heaven. Don't listen to fear, listen to the Holy Spirit and let Him reassure you.

MAY 31ST

Something to take hold of

For in the day of trouble, he will keep me secretly in his pavilion. In the secret place of his tabernacle, he will hide me. He will lift me up on a rock. [6] Now my head will be lifted up above my enemies around me. I will offer sacrifices of joy in his tent. I will sing, yes, I will sing praises to the LORD.

(Psalm 27:5-6)

Remember Psalm 91 where God shows us that we need to be in relationship with Him and speaking out our trust in Him in order to live under His protection? When we are doing that, God promises that He will hide us secretly in Him when trouble comes along. He will lift us up on a rock which cannot be moved, which is a picture of Jesus Himself. Then we will be able to look down on anything and everything that would try to come against us.

Imagine yourself in God's safe place, high upon a rock and looking down on your enemies knowing yourself to be safe in Jesus. Then you will not fear, but will sing praises of joy to your Lord.

JUNE 1ST

Something to declare

The LORD is my shepherd; I shall lack nothing.
(Psalm 23:1)

Today, we're starting to go through Psalm 23. I remember having to learn this by heart in my Church of England primary school. Little did I know how special it was going to be to me many years later.

We looked at some verses from John 10 earlier in the year, where Jesus describes Himself as the shepherd and us as His sheep. Here the psalmist speaks as one of His sheep saying, "The Lord is my shepherd." That's our declaration too. Jesus is our shepherd, watching over us, protecting us and providing us with everything we need. With Jesus as my shepherd I truly shall lack nothing, so fear, you have no place in me.

JUNE 2ND

Something to know

He makes me lie down in green pastures. He leads me beside still waters.
(Psalm 23:2)

Jesus, my shepherd, provides all my needs and a safe place for me to rest in. Knowing this is the way of peace, not fear.

June 3rd

Something to understand

He restores my soul. He guides me in the paths of righteousness for his name's sake.

(Psalm 23:3)

When my thoughts and my emotions are battered and fearful, He restores me to His peace if I turn to Him in faith. He has made me righteous and shows me the way to go which will keep me in His plan for my life. He does it, not because I have earned it, but because Jesus has made it all possible through His death and resurrection; and God will always honour the name of His Son.

June 4th

Something to comfort you

Even though I walk through the valley of the shadow of death, I will fear no evil, for you are with me. Your rod and your staff, they comfort me.

(Psalm 23:4)

I understand that there is a deep, narrow canyon in Israel called 'The Shadow of Death.' The sun can only shine in it at midday when it is right overhead. Presumably the shepherd David who wrote this psalm, had to take his flock through it sometimes. The sheep would have been frightened by the place and not want to go through. Normally a shepherd in biblical times would lead their sheep from the front and the sheep would follow, but they were too afraid to follow him through this valley, so he had to go behind them and urge them forward. He would have done this by tapping them on their backs with his rod and his staff so they would know he was still there and following them. He was comforting them.

This is a picture of God comforting and reassuring us when we go through our valleys of death and are tempted to fear. We may not always feel we can see God, but He reassures us He is still there with us – we do not need to fear even in the most difficult places. God is faithful and will never leave us.

JUNE 5TH

Something to enjoy

You prepare a table before me in the presence of my enemies. You anoint my head with oil. My cup runs over.
(Psalm 23:5)

God is so good. He has only good things for us. It is helpful to know that one day all things will come to light and God's justice will be done as our enemies see our reward.

God anoints our head with oil. This is something that shepherds used to do. They put oil on the horns of their sheep so they would slide off each other when they were fighting so they wouldn't damage each other. Think of the oil on your head when people and situations come against you and let the hurt slide off you.

My cup runs over – just four words, but a wonderfully powerful picture. God's blessings more than fill you, they are so abundant that you can bless others with the blessings you have received. When things are difficult don't fear; imagine the blessings of God overflowing from you. It is what is happening in the spiritual realm. Believe it and receive them into your life.

Instead of fearing people who hurt you, pray for them and ask God if there is any way you can bless them out of the abundance of your blessings. Repaying hurt with kindness can often defuse a situation and put things right.

June 6th

Something to declare

Surely goodness and loving kindness shall follow me all the days of my life, and I will dwell in the LORD's house forever.
(Psalm 23:6)

We come to the last verse of Psalm 23 and what a great ending.

God doesn't say that bad things won't happen, but He promises that His goodness and loving-kindness is with us whatever else is happening. When all around you is screaming the opposite; when all you can see and hear is evil and hurt, declare this verse out loud with conviction and authority. Ask God to open your eyes so you can see His goodness and loving-kindness following you. Go to the Bible and build yourself up in His love for you and His promises for your future in this life and the next. You will be with Jesus forever. Hallelujah!

Fear will be cast out when you truly take hold of God's goodness and His loving-kindness.

June 7th

Something to understand

"Listen to me, you who know righteousness, the people in whose heart is my law. Don't fear the reproach of men, and don't be dismayed at their insults. [8] For the moth will eat them up like a garment, and the worm will eat them like wool; but my righteousness will be forever, and my salvation to all generations."

(Isaiah 51:7-8)

Isaiah is talking to those who know righteousness and have God's law in their heart. If you have made Jesus your Lord and Saviour, then you have been made righteous through His death and resurrection And if you also love God's Word and have a true desire to live by it, then these words of Isaiah are for you.

He tells the people not to fear what men may say to them – words of accusation, condemnation, anger, confrontation etc. Things may be really difficult now, but refuse to fear, and look at the long-term outlook. Those who reject Jesus are heading for hell and you are on your way to heaven. The reproaches of men will not last for ever, but your righteousness and salvation will. Praise God!

JUNE 8TH

<u>Something to grasp hold of</u>

For we are his workmanship, created in Christ Jesus for good works, which God prepared before that we would walk in them.
(Ephesians 2:10)

We are made by God! Psalm 139:13 tells us that God created us in our mother's womb. And 2 Corinthians 5:17 tells us that now we are born-again, we are a new creation. God has given us a brand-new perfect spirit. When you feel insignificant or a failure or someone else says negative things about you, remember – you are God's workmanship, created in Christ Jesus.

When there is so much negativity around about what is happening and what might happen, it is so easy to start to fear. But get hold of the fact that God has a plan for your life and that it is a good plan. Ask Him to show you what it is and wait in faith for Him to show you the next step forward.

Replace fear with the knowledge of who you are in Jesus – a new creation. Hallelujah!

June 9th

Something to declare

I will not die, but live, and declare the LORD's works.
(Psalm 118:17)

Refuse to accept defeat. It can be hard sometimes when things are difficult, but speak out your faith and declare in the face of fear, "I will not die, but live, and declare the LORD's works."

JUNE 10TH

Something to put into practice

I know this: that God is for me. [10] In God, I will praise his word. In the LORD, I will praise his word.
(Psalm 56:9-10)

Let's look at just four verses from Psalm 56. Here are the first two.

Do you know that God isn't against you and He isn't neutral about you – He is for you; He is actively on your side. If you are born-again then this is true whether you feel it or not. The Lord God Almighty is for you. Isn't that a reason to start praising Him for the truth of His Word! Where there is true praise, fear is silenced. Thank You Lord!

June 11th

Something to declare

I have put my trust in God. I will not be afraid. What can man do to me?

(Psalm 56:11)

The psalmist continues with another declaration. He says he has put his trust in God and therefore He will not be afraid. What man can do to you, however difficult that may be to experience, pales into insignificance when we know God is on our side.

Speak this out and confirm it in your mind and your heart so its truth is firmly established there, ready for you to stand on when necessary. You are arming yourself against fear before it comes. Remember, you prepare for war in times of peace.

June 12TH

<u>Something to remember</u>

For you have delivered my soul from death, and prevented my feet from falling, that I may walk before God in the light of the living.
(Psalm 56:13)

When everything seems hopeless, look back at what God has done in your life. He has saved you from despair and hell. His angels have kept you from falling and hurting yourself. He did this not so you could be fearful again, but so that you can walk forward living your life with Him surrounded by the light of His love and goodness.

Don't give in to despair, speak out loud all the ways God has saved you in the past and thank Him that he's going to do it again. He is faithful.

These are four powerful verses that we have looked at from this psalm. May they help you to stand and keep standing in the face of fear. They are verses that have certainly helped me.

JUNE 13TH

Something to determine

I have been crucified with Christ, and it is no longer I who live, but Christ lives in me. That life which I now live in the flesh, I live by faith in the Son of God, who loved me and gave himself up for me.

(Galatians 2:20)

When Jesus was crucified, our old sinful nature was crucified with Him. This becomes a reality in our lives when we are born-again. I can hear you saying, "But I still sin, I still get things wrong." I know – so do I. But we have to take on board the fact that our old nature is dead and that in its place we have a brand-new perfect spirit. Determine to think and live in that truth.

Because it's dead, your old nature no longer has any power over you. So, when you are tempted to sin, you can now say "No," and when you do sin, you can receive the forgiveness that Jesus has won for you. Don't think of yourself as a sinner – that can lead to worry and anxiety. Instead, know that your old sin nature was crucified with Jesus and you now have a spirit that is just like Jesus's.

Let's determine to live our lives by faith in Jesus who did it all because of His great love for us.

June 14th

Something to declare

As for me, I will call on God. The LORD will save me.
(Psalm 55:16)

There are so many powerful declarations for us to make our own in the psalms. Here's another one.

All sorts of difficult and fearful things may be going on in your life or around you BUT let's refuse to entertain fear and say, "As for me, I will call on God. The Lord will save me."

If you are struggling to believe this, then look back at the verses through the year so far. They are God's Word. Remember, faith comes by hearing and hearing by the word of God (Romans 10:17). So keep speaking them out and as you hear them, your faith will rise and you will be able to declare this with true conviction and authority.

JUNE 15TH

Something to take hold of

On that day, when evening had come, he said to them,
"Let's go over to the other side." 36 Leaving the multitude,
they took him with them, even as he was, in the boat.
Other small boats were also with him. 37 A big wind storm
arose, and the waves beat into the boat, so much that the
boat was already filled. 38 He himself was in the stern,
asleep on the cushion; and they woke him up and asked
him, "Teacher, don't you care that we are dying?" 39 He
awoke and rebuked the wind, and said to the sea, "Peace!
Be still!" The wind ceased and there was a great calm. 40 He
said to them, "Why are you so afraid? How is it that you
have no faith?"

(Mark 4:35-40)

Jesus told His disciples that they were going to the other side of the lake. He settled in the back of the boat and went to sleep. A violent storm then arose and the disciples were afraid they were going to drown. They woke Jesus and, after He had stilled the storm, He asked them this question, "Why are you so afraid? How is it that you have no faith?"

When everything around them was out of control, they completely forgot that Jesus had said they were going to the other side. They had put no faith in what He had said. If they had, they would have been able to encourage each other saying, "If Jesus says we'll get to the other side, then we will. Let's just keep going." When things around us are trying to make us fear, let's encourage ourselves and others with God's Word. Don't let's be afraid. If God says so, then it shall be so. Let's just keep going no matter what.

JUNE 16TH

<u>Something to act upon</u>

And let the peace of God rule in your hearts.
(Colossians 3:15)

Here is another verse that I've learnt to rely on. We all face situations in our lives when it's really hard to make a decision. We toss various scenarios around in our minds and the more we think about the possible consequences of making the wrong decision, the more fearful and anxious we become. God has the solution. He says to let His peace rule in our hearts.

When you can't decide between two courses of action, imagine yourself having chosen each of them in turn and see which scenario gives you the most peace. It may not come straightaway, but give it time. When you do this, you are letting peace be the umpire – peace is giving the ruling over what to do. You are letting the peace of God rule in your heart and you can go forward confidently instead of in fear.

JUNE 17TH

Something to look forward to

"In my Father's house are many homes. If it weren't so, I would have told you. I am going to prepare a place for you. [3] If I go and prepare a place for you, I will come again and will receive you to myself; that where I am, you may be there also."

(John 14:2-3)

Jesus told us that in this world we will have trouble, but we have a world beyond imagining to look forward to when this life is over. Jesus says that He is preparing a home for us in heaven. Other translations call it a mansion. It's not going to be a shoe box that is barely adequate. It's going to be amazing – God is the perfect architect, planner, builder and interior designer!

When things are difficult here and now, and fear tries to take hold, take some time to see yourself in heaven, living a life far above the best that this life can offer in every way. When you die, or if Jesus comes back first, He will take you there and you will enjoy it for eternity with Him.

June 18th

Something to stand on

"Be strong and courageous. Don't be afraid or dismayed because of the king of Assyria, nor for all the multitude who is with him; for there is a greater one with us than with him."

(2 Chronicles 32:7)

These words were spoken by King Hezekiah, one of the kings of Judah in Old Testament times. They were facing a battle against the king of Assyria and the people were afraid because his army was so big. But they had an advantage Assyria did not – they had God with them and that made all the difference.

If you are facing a big battle in some way, and everything seems to be stacked against you, remember – God is on your side and He will be with you. Silence fear with praise and thanks to Him and go forward in faith.

JUNE 19TH

Something to put into practice

For thus said the Lord GOD, the Holy One of Israel, "You will be saved in returning and rest. Your strength will be in quietness and in confidence."

(Isaiah 30:15)

When we're in a tight squeeze it can be very easy to use up our mental and emotional energy very quickly. Fear really saps your strength. God says to turn our focus on Him and rest in His love for us and presence with us. When we quieten our thoughts and emotions in Him and put all our trust in Him, then He will give us the strength we need to work through the problem and come out the other side intact.

JUNE 20TH

Something to understand

Having stripped the principalities and the powers, he made a show of them openly, triumphing over them in it.
(Colossians 2:15)

This is what Jesus did on the Cross. The principalities and powers are the devil and all His demons. Jesus won the victory over them, utterly defeating them, so that the only way they can try to harm us now is through us if we fall for their lies.

In Roman days, when a criminal was executed, his body was tied behind a chariot and dragged along the streets of the city. This sounds terribly gruesome to us today but there was a point to it. The authorities wanted the people to know for sure that the person they had feared was really dead and they had no need to fear him anymore.

Jesus made an open show of his defeat of the devil so we would know for sure that there is absolutely no reason for us to fear him anymore. He triumphed over the devil and all his demons. Make a decision today to never fear the devil again. And if ever you're tempted to do so, cast those thoughts down and start thanking and praising Jesus for His total victory over him.

June 21st

Something to take hold of

Those who love your law have great peace. Nothing causes them to stumble.

(Psalm 119:165)

This verse is in the Old Testament, but as believers in Jesus, we can take 'the law' to mean God's Word. Do you love God's Word? Is it more important to you than anything else? Those are challenging questions for us all. But God assures us that when we love His Word and make it the basis for how we live our lives, we have great peace.

Maybe you're not finding this is your experience. But that doesn't stop it being true. Take hold of this verse today. Choose to believe it is true. Thank God for His peace – He's already given it to you. Open your heart to it and allow it to fill you. Keep going in your faith in His Word and nothing will make you stumble. The peace of God is far greater than any fear.

JUNE 22ND

Something to rejoice about

... through whom we also have our access by faith into this grace in which we stand. We rejoice in hope of the glory of God.

(Romans 5:2)

It is all because of Jesus that we can stand in the grace of God – we don't deserve it and we couldn't earn any of it. It is God's unconditional love poured out on us and in us. We simply enjoy it and rejoice in Him, knowing that one day we will not only see Him in all His glory, but share in it too. What a future! Tell fear that you stand in the grace of God and are heading for glory and it will be silenced.

June 23rd

Something to take on board

Not only this, but we also rejoice in our sufferings, knowing that suffering produces perseverance; [4] and perseverance, proven character; and proven character, hope; [5] and hope doesn't disappoint us, because God's love has been poured into our hearts through the Holy Spirit who was given to us.

(Romans 5:3-5)

Paul continues in these three verses. They are quite challenging. When we are persecuted for our faith, rather than focusing on hurt and fear, we are told to rejoice because persecution can change us for the better.

When we suffer for Jesus we have to persevere, staying faithful to Him. And this in turn makes our character stronger and more steadfast. And when we have a strong character which refuses to buckle under persecution, then we know that we have a certain hope in Jesus for the here and now and for eternity. This hope isn't an attitude of seeing what happens and hoping it will be ok. Hope in the Bible is a certain expectation and that will not disappoint.

We have the love of God poured into our hearts and the Holy Spirit living within us to teach, guide and encourage us. How can fear stand against that?

June 24th

Something to decide

For the mind of the flesh is death, but the mind of the Spirit is life and peace; 7 because the mind of the flesh is hostile towards God, for it is not subject to God's law, neither indeed can it be. 8 Those who are in the flesh can't please God. 9 But you are not in the flesh but in the Spirit, if it is so that the Spirit of God dwells in you.

(Romans 8:6-9)

In these verses, Paul contrasts those who are not born-again with those who are. Those who aren't have no choice but to live according to their own ideas and desires, the flesh, so they can never please God. Those who are born-again, have the Spirit of God living within them and so are able to please God.

There is also a finer distinction here. It is possible to be born-again but live according to the flesh and not the Spirit. Is that you? Even though you have given your life to Jesus, do you still do your own thing and make your own decisions without a thought of God's Word and His ways? If you do, there will inevitably be times when you feel fear. Peace comes only by having your mind focused on God and His Holy Spirit.

Decide to start to think according to the Spirit, not your flesh. Get into God's Word and ask the Holy Spirit who lives in you to help you understand it. He will. And you will find that peace will replace your fear.

June 25th

Something to declare

Why are you in despair, my soul? Why are you disturbed within me? Hope in God! For I shall still praise him for the saving help of his presence.

(Psalm 42:5)

We read a similar verse to this earlier in the year. In fact, it starts with the same questions. The psalmist talks to his own mind and emotions and asks them why they are in despair and disturbed. I'm sure we have all had times in our lives when we have felt despair and our thoughts have been in turmoil. It's a horrible place to be and there is real fear in it. Well, read on, because he then tells us what to do to get out of that place.

He tells his thoughts and emotions to put their faith in God. You can't ask God to change the way you think and feel, and then just carry on in the same way waiting for Him to do it. He won't bypass your free will. He's told us how to change our thoughts and emotions. We have to take responsibility for them.

The psalmist says that he will STILL praise God. We need to determine to still praise God. Praising Him is a powerful way to turn our thoughts and emotions around. After all, He is the only One who can truly help us and save us and He is the only One who is ALWAYS with us.

Make this your declaration today and see fear disappear and certain hope rise.

JUNE 26TH

Something to declare

I will lift up my eyes to the hills. Where does my help come from? [2] My help comes from the LORD, who made heaven and earth.

(Psalm 121:1-2)

We can get so bogged down in our problems and all the possible scenarios that might or might not happen. When you find yourself swamped by fear and anxiety, it's time to stop and look up. You may not have hills near you, but we can all see the sky. Remember that God is the One who made the whole earth with all its complexity and grandeur. Who else would you turn to than the creator of all. Declare with the psalmist that your help comes from God and believe it is on its way – it will come. Thank You Lord.

June 27th

Something to realise

The LORD is on my side amongst those who help me.
(Psalm 118:7)

I've said before in this book that God is on our side and His desire is to help us and strengthen us and encourage us and fight for us and so much more. God loves to work through people and sometimes we fail to recognise His help because it doesn't appear to come directly from Him. I remember a story that you may have heard also.

A man has got into difficulties in the sea and is drowning. He calls out to God for help and believes that God will answer and save him. A canoeist comes by and offers him a life jacket but the man refuses it because God is going to save him. Then a helicopter appears and a ladder is thrown down for him to climb to safety, but again he says no because God is going to save him. Finally, someone swims out to him and tells him to climb on his back and he will get him to safety. But still the man refuses. Eventually he drowns. When he gets to heaven, he asks God why He hadn't come to save him. God replies, "I sent you a canoe and a helicopter and a swimmer but you refused all my help."

When we call out to God in fear, He will usually use other people to help us. Let's realise that He is on our side amongst those who help us and be thankful.

June 28th

Something to put into practice

My son, let them not depart from your eyes. Keep sound wisdom and discretion, [22] so they will be life to your soul, and grace for your neck.

(Proverbs 3:21-22)

We end this month with four verses from Proverbs 3. Here are the first two. The writer is talking about the Word of God. He tells us to keep it in our sight. In other words, keep God's Word before you in the front of your mind all the time. That might sound impossible, but if God tells you to do something, it is possible.

I have learnt over the years that the more I read and think on God's Word the more it does stay in the front of my mind. Even when I'm concentrating on something else entirely, I find it there guiding me and helping me. I'm not perfect at this, but I have found it has got easier the more I've focused on His Word.

We need sound wisdom and discretion so much in our world. Keep God's truth ready in your thinking for when you need it. It will give you life, not fear, and you will know God's unconditional and sacrificial love for you throughout the day.

June 29th

<u>Something to understand</u>

Then you shall walk in your way securely. Your foot won't stumble.

(Proverbs 3:23)

Notice that this verse begins with 'Then'. It links what it says back to yesterday's verses. When we keep God's Word in the front of our minds, we will more easily be able to discern what is right and what is wrong and which way to go. This will give us confidence to walk forward securely, free from fear and without stumbling.

June 30th

Something to take on board

When you lie down, you will not be afraid. Yes, you will lie down, and your sleep will be sweet.
(Proverbs 3:24)

What a lovely way to end the first half of the year – with the promise of sweet sleep. Once again, this verse links back to verses 21-22.

If you have spent the day looking at the way the world sees things, then those images will be stored in your mind and your heart, and your sleep will probably not be sweet. Have you ever watched the news at night and seen and heard all the grim happenings and all the dire forecasts of what might happen, and then wondered why you've slept badly? Maybe it's time to make some adjustments to what you 'keep before your eyes'.

We all know that things that are difficult in the day can seem alarmingly fearful in the middle of the night. But if you have stored God's Word up in your mind and in your heart, then it is there for you in the night and you do not need to be afraid when you lie down to sleep. You can meditate on all God's love for you and His powerful promises and rest easily, assured of your safety in him. Sweet dreams.

JULY 1ST

Something to understand

"By faith in his name, his name has made this man strong, whom you see and know. Yes, the faith which is through him has given him this perfect soundness in the presence of you all."
(Acts 3:16)

Peter and John had just healed a man who had been unable to walk from birth. He was now on his feet walking, leaping and praising God. The people who saw him were amazed and Peter explained to them how this miracle had happened. It was all to do with the man's faith in Jesus. The power is Jesus's, but the faith to take hold of it is ours.

Jesus often said to people that their faith had made them well. We want the responsibility to be on someone else, but when you think about it, it's good news that it's ours. If it was a matter of waiting for God to act, then we could do nothing about it. But if it's down to us, then we can get on and do something.

Remember, you have the gift of faith from God, and Jesus says that even a small amount is powerful enough to move mountains. The issue is, do you have any doubt and unbelief alongside your faith? Are you afraid that God may heal others but He won't do it for you? Are you unsure if God even wants you well? Declare out loud the truth that Jesus has already won your healing and knock unbelief and fear on the head. Then your faith can rise and you can receive your healing. Thank God for it before you see it and refuse to allow fear and doubt back in, however long it takes.

July 2nd

Something to declare

The LORD is my light and my salvation. Whom shall I fear? The LORD is the strength of my life. Of whom shall I be afraid?

(Psalm 27:1)

Jesus has won our salvation for us and He is our light, showing us the way forward. He is also our strength. We don't have to do things in our own way, relying only on ourselves or others.

Think about it. God Himself has saved you and is showing you the way to go and giving you the strength to do it. Why then would we ever fear? In the light of that, how can anything man might do or say make us afraid?

But we know that fear can easily sneak in and when we start to listen to it, it can overwhelm us so we lose sight of God and who He is. That's why it's important to keep making declarations of faith to build ourselves up in the truth and keep us focused on Him. Make this verse your own declaration today and let its truth become a part of who you are.

JULY 3RD

Something to take on board

We are therefore ambassadors on behalf of Christ.
(2 Corinthians 5:20)

The Google dictionary says an ambassador is 'an accredited diplomat sent by a state as its permanent representative in a foreign country.' That's who we are. Jesus has authorised us and equipped us and sent us out to represent Him in the world. And yes, the world is a foreign country to those of us who follow Jesus. It is ruled by man's ways and we belong to the Kingdom of God.

Don't let the devil frighten you with his lies about being inadequate. Jesus has called you to an important role and He has given you everything you need to fulfil it. And it's a permanent role; He's not going to take it away from you. He says you are His ambassador and so you are.

So don't be afraid – lift your head up and make the decision today not to fear, but to walk confidently in the truth of who you are in Jesus and what He has called you to do.

JULY 4TH

Something to know

LORD, you will ordain peace for us, for you have also done all our work for us.

(Isaiah 26:12)

Jesus has already done everything that is needed for us to live free from fear. There is nothing for us to do except believe on Jesus and accept Him as our Lord and Saviour. When we stand with Him in confidence, and trust Him in all the problems of life, big and small, then it isn't fear that will fill us, but the peace of God. Praise Him!

July 5th

Something to reassure you

For whom he foreknew, he also predestined to be conformed to the image of his Son, that he might be the firstborn amongst many brothers. 30 Whom he predestined, those he also called. Whom he called, those he also justified. Whom he justified, those he also glorified.

(Romans 8:29-30)

God has always known there would be a you. This doesn't mean that He intentionally caused you as an individual to come into being. If He did that with every baby that is born, He would have to organise rape and incest as well as happy families. He created the principle of life being conceiving when a sperm fertilises an egg; we are the ones who decide whether to make a baby or not. But he has always known of every single individual person who would be born.

And He has always known who would accept Jesus and who would not. He didn't pick who to save and who not to. He gave us free will so we could choose for ourselves, but He knew which choice we would all make. God never predestined anyone to hell, but He did predestine those who would be born-again to become like Jesus. His Holy Spirit lives inside us, united with our perfect brand-new spirit, and so we are made in the image of Jesus.

He then called those He predestined, and justified them when they gave their life to Him. He made us 'just as if we had never sinned' through Jesus's sacrifice. Don't worry about whether God has chosen you or not. You choose Jesus and follow Him, knowing that God always knew you would be His.

July 6th

Something to realise

He teaches my hands to war, so that my arms bend a bow of bronze.

(Psalm 18:34)

In the Old Testament, God's people had to fight a lot of battles. Here David gives God the glory for His physical strength which helps him to win when he fights.

Our battles are not likely to be physical, but God has still given us His strength to fight the enemy – the devil. When you're tempted to fear and feel overwhelmed by the battles you face, be like David and thank God for the strength He has given you in Jesus to enable you to fight on and win.

July 7th

Something to stand on

I looked, and rose up, and said to the nobles, to the rulers, and to the rest of the people, "Don't be afraid of them! Remember the LORD, who is great and awesome, and fight for your brothers, your sons, your daughters, your wives, and your houses."
(Nehemiah 4:14)

Nehemiah is rebuilding the walls of Jerusalem, but he is coming under attack. He speaks to those who are helping him, telling them not to be afraid of those who are against them. He tells them to remember who is on their side – the great and awesome God. He then encourages them to keep going not only for their own sake, but for the sake of their families and their houses, all of which will be much safer once the walls have been rebuilt.

Don't waste time worrying – it will only sap your strength; just get on with what God has called you to do. Remember, it will benefit others around you as well as yourself. Use that as an incentive to reject fear and press forward no matter what anyone else may say or do. The great and awesome God is with you – what else can you want!

JULY 8TH

Something to take hold of

Don't you be afraid, for I am with you. Don't be dismayed, for I am your God. I will strengthen you. Yes, I will help you. Yes, I will uphold you with the right hand of my righteousness.

(Isaiah 41:10)

God assures His people that He is with them so they do not need to be dismayed. He speaks these words to us today as well. Read this verse slowly, dwelling on each truth and letting it settle into your mind and your heart. The Almighty God is with you. He will strengthen you. He will help you. He upholds you with His right hand of power, strength and righteousness. Thank You Lord.

July 9th

Something to declare

Being therefore justified by faith, we have peace with God through our Lord Jesus Christ.

(Romans 5:1)

Here is that word 'justified' again. We have been made just as if we had never sinned; washed completely clean. How did it happen? Jesus played His part – He took the punishment for our sins so we could be forgiven. And we played our part – in faith we received all that Jesus had done and won for us.

And the end result is peace with God – He's not angry with us. If you have fear because of something you have done, go back to the foundation of your faith – Jesus's death and resurrection. Praise God for it and all He has done for you and allow His peace to banish fear. Declare out loud – "Being justified by faith, I have peace with God through my Lord Jesus Christ."

July 10th

Something to know

Haven't you known? Haven't you heard? The everlasting God, the LORD, the Creator of the ends of the earth, doesn't faint. He isn't weary. His understanding is unsearchable. [29] He gives power to the weak. He increases the strength of him who has no might.

(Isaiah 40:28-29)

Do you know? Have you heard? The eternal Creator God never gets tired or fed up. He knows everything and He has power for you when you are weak, and strength for you when you have no resources left. Don't fear when you get to the end of yourself – turn to God and receive His power and strength.

July 11th

Something to take on board

You were dead through your trespasses and the uncircumcision of your flesh. He made you alive together with him, having forgiven us all our trespasses, [14] wiping out the handwriting in ordinances which was against us. He has taken it out of the way, nailing it to the cross.

(Colossians 2:13-14)

Everything that you have ever done wrong has been forgiven – the things that seem small and the things that seem huge. And when you are born-again, you can receive that forgiveness in full.

The list of all your sins (past, present and future) which stood against you and caused you to fear, has been wiped out. I imagine it this way: the list of all my sins was written on a piece of paper and nailed to the Cross beneath Jesus as He hung on it. As Jesus suffered the agony of the Cross, His blood flowed down the Cross and onto the list of my sins. It smudged the writing until it became illegible and eventually His blood caused the paper itself to disintegrate. The list was wiped out completely. There is no longer any record of my sins.

You are no longer spiritually dead because of your sins; you are now spiritually alive because of Jesus. Forget what's gone before and the fear that's associated with it, and look to what's ahead with Him.

JULY 12TH

Something to take on board

Pleasant words are a honeycomb, sweet to the soul, and health to the bones.

(Proverbs 16:24)

Do you remember when we read the verse about death and life being in the power of the tongue? It was on March 10th. Here is another verse from Proverbs telling us some of the results of speaking life.

I think you will agree that when someone says pleasant things to you it does you good. But the verse goes on to say pleasant words are also health to your bones.

The medical profession will say that if someone has a positive attitude towards dealing with their illness or condition, they are more likely to have a good outcome. Let's add the power of God onto that. I'm not suggesting you say you aren't ill when you are. I'm saying, don't talk about it with a negative outlook. Silence fear by talking positively, declaring the truth that Jesus has already won your healing for you. And do the same for others. Use pleasant words over yourself and others and allow them to do their work.

JULY 13TH

<u>Something to take hold of</u>

For what if some were without faith? Will their lack of faith nullify the faithfulness of God? May it never be! Yes, let God be found true, but every man a liar.

(Romans 3:3)

Don't listen to the doubting or unbelieving voice of others. Just because someone else says God's Word isn't true doesn't make it untrue. On the contrary, if someone disagrees with God's truth, then it is they who are the liars – never God. When you hear wrong things that can make you fearful, don't allow them to settle in your mind or your heart. God is always true – speak His truth out and let the words of unbelievers and doubters fall useless to the ground.

July 14th

Something to put into practice

"Whoever doesn't receive you or hear your words, as you go out of that house or that city, shake the dust off your feet."

(Matthew 10:14)

This was an instruction Jesus gave to His disciples when He sent them out to tell people about Him and heal the sick. Have you ever talked to someone about Jesus and they just haven't wanted to know? Maybe they've refused to listen or reacted very negatively to what you've said. Maybe they got angry or accused you of interfering in their life. Jesus says to shake their dust off your feet.

The roads in Bible times were just dirt tracks and because the people wore sandals in the heat, their feet got very dusty as they walked along. Jesus said not to carry the dust from a place where they had been rejected and take it with them to the next.

It's not nice when someone rejects the gospel when you try to share it with them. Harsh words can linger in our minds as can a refusal to even listen. And when negative things stay in our minds they can quickly lead to bitterness and fear. Do they hate me? Will they say negative things about me to other people? If only I had said this or that. Jesus says to shake those thoughts out of our minds and hearts and walk on completely free of them. Don't give bitterness, hurt and fear a place to grow. Praise God that no matter what others may say, His gospel remains the truth. Shake the dust off your feet and continue on your way with Jesus.

July 15th

Something to know

God was in Christ reconciling the world to himself, not reckoning to them their trespasses, and having committed to us the word of reconciliation.
(2 Corinthians 5:19)

This is what God was doing through Jesus – not judging us, but reconciling us to Him. God is perfect and cannot have sin in His presence, yet He loved us so much and longed to be in relationship with us. It sounds impossible to resolve. But God had the answer. Instead of punishing us for our sins, He put our sins on Jesus and punished Him for them instead of us. Now, when we accept what Jesus did for us personally and receive Him as our Lord and Saviour, we are washed clean of all those sins – we can receive complete forgiveness and come into relationship with our Father God. We are reconciled to Him.

So many people are crippled by fear when they think of all they've done that is wrong. God can't possibly love me; God can't possibly use me; I'm sure I will go to hell when I die. Know today for absolutely certain – God does love you. He loves you so much that He sacrificed His own Son so He wouldn't have to sacrifice you. God has a plan for your life and longs to use you. And if you are born-again, there is no way you are going to hell; you are going to spend eternity with Jesus in glory because He has reconciled you to God forever. How can fear stand in the face of that!

JULY 16TH

Something to realise

The fear of the LORD is the beginning of wisdom.
(Proverbs 9:10)

Today we look at a verse which mentions fear, but which uses the word in a completely different way. When the Bible talks about the fearing God, it doesn't mean being frightened of Him. Everything we've looked at through this book shows us that, as believers, we do not need to fear Him in that way at all. The fear mentioned in this verse is an old use of the word, meaning to hold Him in awe and respect.

When we have respect for God and hold Him in awe, we will want to listen to what He says in His Word and through His Holy Spirit, and we will then find His wisdom that we need to make good decisions day by day. Don't be frightened of God. Turn to Him through Jesus. Hold Him in awe and respect Him. Then you will start to find true wisdom.

JULY 17TH

Something to put into practice

Don't be wise in your own eyes. Fear the LORD, and depart from evil. [8] It will be health to your body, and nourishment to your bones.

(Proverbs 3:7-8)

We all have a choice when we need to make a decision about how to go forward. We can try to work it out for ourselves by listening to what the world has to say and by reacting according to how we feel, or we can turn to God's wisdom with awe and respect for Him and His Word.

We might get things right by ourselves once in a while, but if we carry on doing it our way, the ultimate result will be a mess, and that's a recipe for fear.

But doing it His way will not only help you make the right decisions; His Word will actually give you health and strength. Why would you choose your way with fear and failure, when you can choose God's way with health and strength. Go for it with God and see the difference it will make.

July 18th

Something to rejoice about

But you, LORD, are a shield around me, my glory, and the one who lifts up my head. [4] I cry to the LORD with my voice, and he answers me out of his holy hill.

(Psalm 3:3-4)

When you live your life in relationship with God, He protects you like a shield around your body. He gives you His glory – the shining light of His goodness. And He lifts up your head.

How often have you been downcast with your shoulders slumped and your head bowed down in fear and despair? We've all been there at some time. But God wants to lift your head up – He wants to set you above your enemies, above every situation that would try to beat you down. He's the only One who can really do it. Cry to Him and thank Him for being a shield around you and for sharing His glory with you. He will hear you and lift your head. Thank You Lord.

July 19th

Something to put into practice

Finally, brothers, rejoice! Be perfected. Be comforted. Be of the same mind. Live in peace, and the God of love and peace will be with you.
(2 Corinthians 13:11)

Paul has been writing to the church at Corinth with instructions about how to live for Jesus, and finally he comes to this verse. First, He says to rejoice. Then He says to be perfected. I can imagine you saying, "But I thought it wasn't about me, I thought it was all about receiving what Jesus has done for me." You're right – it is. But remember, although you have a brand-new perfect spirit within you, your mind and heart are not perfected yet. So allow your spirit to influence your thoughts, words and actions. The job's been done in your spirit. Now let your perfect spirit start to influence your thoughts, emotions, attitudes and even your body.

And be comforted. What lovely words. Are you feeling sorrowful, fearful, inadequate, ashamed? Be comforted – Jesus has won your freedom from all these things so you can step into it.

Understand God's truth and His ways and encourage others to do so too. Then you can be of the same mind with them, not in compromise, but in agreement in the truth of God. Try to live in peace with people as far as you can from your side, especially other believers.

Seek to do all this and fear will be silenced, and you will experience the love and peace which is already yours through Jesus.

July 20th

Something to reassure you

What then shall we say about these things? If God is for us, who can be against us?
(Romans 8:31)

God is on our side. He says this quite a few times through His Word – He really wants us to get hold of it. In this letter, Paul has mentioned the sufferings of this life and the persecution that comes through following Jesus. Do we spend our time talking about such things? Do we grumble about them with everyone we meet? Are we going to get into fear over them? Paul asks the question, "What then shall we say about these things?" Answer – let's make our answer, "Nothing." Let's stop saying all the negative stuff – God is on our side, so what does it matter if someone is against us. Fear, you have no hold on me. I declare that God Himself is on my side. Hallelujah!"

JULY 21ST

Something to take on board

We were buried therefore with him through baptism into death, that just as Christ was raised from the dead through the glory of the Father, so we also might walk in newness of life.

(Romans 6:4)

We've already talked about how our old nature was put to death with Jesus on the Cross. It is now dead and buried. And just as Jesus was raised from the dead, so are we, but it's not our old nature that was raised with all its sin and fear – no, it's our new nature that is raised, having been made perfect in Jesus, and fear has no place in it.

When things go against you, don't try and raise your old nature back to life. We have a new life to live now we have been born-again. The old is dead and buried. The new is alive and well. Thank You Jesus.

JULY 22ND

Something to act upon

Strengthen the weak hands, and make the feeble knees firm. [4] Tell those who have a fearful heart, "Be strong! Don't be afraid!"

(Isaiah 35:3-4)

When we've strengthened our own hands and knees with God's truth and with the praise of God, then we can help and encourage others. We can tell those who are afraid, to be strong. Just like Paul and Silas, others can greatly benefit by our attitude when things are difficult.

July 23rd

Something to understand

We know that all things work together for good for those who love God, for those who are called according to his purpose.

(Romans 8:28)

This is a verse that can easily be misunderstood leading to seriously wrong thinking of the way God works. He isn't controlling everything that happens. It isn't a case of what will be will be. If it was, there would be no point in praying or seeking God's will and wisdom. Look back at January 17th. If it's good it's from God; if it's bad it's from the devil. God has given us all free will and we reap the results of our wrong choices as individuals and nations.

Some translations make the meaning of this verse clearer by saying that in all things God works for the good of those who love him, who have been called according to his purpose. When we love God and are seeking to live His way, we can be confident that He will bring good out of even the bad things that happen to us.

When something bad happens to you, don't spiral down into despair, panic and fear. Cast your negative thoughts down and tell God you love Him. Thank Him for His promise that He will bring good out of it and wait in faith. He will not disappoint.

July 24TH

Something to put into practice

"Again, assuredly I tell you, that if two of you will agree on earth concerning anything that they will ask, it will be done for them by my Father who is in heaven."
(Matthew 18:19)

What a powerful verse this is and one, I suggest, that is not applied very often. God doesn't need lots of people praying to persuade Him to answer you. He isn't a reluctant God – He's a generous God who wants to bless you more than you want to be blessed.

Refuse to listen to fear telling you that God won't answer your prayer. Make a decision to stand on all His promises in the faith He has given you. He will hear you and answer you.

If you feel you need prayer support, instead of asking a lot of people to pray, follow the directions of Jesus in this verse. Choose a Christian you can trust who you know will stand in faith with you, trusting God and His Word. Pray together and know it will be done. There is no need to use lots of words or keep asking again and again. Take hold of what this verse promises; cast fear down and determine to wait in faith for His answer – it will come. Jesus assures you of this and He is faithful to His Word.

July 25th

Something to put into practice

Everyone helps his neighbour. They say to their brothers, "Be strong!"
(Isaiah 41:6)

God delights to work through people. We can probably all remember times when He has encouraged us through someone else. But it works both ways. Sometimes God wants to use us to help someone else not to fear, but to be strong. Thank You Lord for using me.

JULY 26TH

Something to determine

I laid myself down and slept. I awakened, for the LORD sustains me. [6] I will not be afraid of tens of thousands of people who have set themselves against me on every side.

(Psalm 3:5-6)

We all know how bleak and black things can seem in the middle of the night and how easy it is for fear to overwhelm us. But even when we are battling with a difficult situation and everything seems to be against us, we can still sleep well when we know that the Lord sustains us. He is on your side and has already won the battle. Stand with Him and you stand on the side that's already won.

Declare your complete trust in Him as your refuge and your fortress and the One who keeps you going, and sleep well.

JULY 27TH

Something to realise

In peace I will both lay myself down and sleep, for you alone, the LORD, make me live in safety.

(Psalm 4:8)

When all your trust is in the Lord and only in Him, then, rather than tossing about all night in fear, you can sleep in peace knowing He will keep you safe.

July 28th

Something to declare

Though an army should encamp against me, my heart shall not fear. Though war should rise against me, even then I will be confident.

(Psalm 27:3)

This is another battle verse – one to declare out loud when you're really up against it. Put your confidence in God your Father, in all His promises and in all Jesus has done and won for you. That will silence fear and you will see the victory.

July 29th

Something to rejoice about

He has redeemed my soul in peace from the battle that was against me, although there are many who oppose me.
(Psalm 55:18)

When everything is lined up against us and the battle is raging, we need to make the decision to put our trust in Him and refuse to be moved from it. Only by doing that will fear be silenced so we can experience the peace of God in the middle of it all. Cast fear down and allow His perfect peace into your thoughts and your emotions. Praise You Lord!

July 30th

Something to take hold of

For I, the LORD your God, will hold your right hand, saying to you, 'Don't be afraid. I will help you.'
(Isaiah 41:13)

As born-again Christians, we are never alone. When we feel alone, it's not true. Don't trust how you feel – that's an open door to fear. Trust the Word of God with all its promises – that's an open door to peace. He has promised to never leave you or forsake you.

Listen to what He's saying to you in this verse. His hand is held out towards you. Put your hand in His and leave it there. Don't be afraid; He will help you in everything you face.

July 31st

<u>Something to decide on</u>

So then, let's follow after things which make for peace, and things by which we may build one another up.
(Romans 14:19)

I think everyone would like peace in their lives. But it's no good just muddling along, going with your feelings, and hoping fear will eventually go away and God's peace will arrive one day.

As a born-again Christian, you have His peace in you. Choose to believe it and let it flow into your thoughts and your emotions by focusing on His Word and thinking about His good things. When you're built up in the peace of God, you can bring His peace into the situations around you where others will allow it. You can then help them not to be fearful too, and encourage them to follow the way of God's peace in their own lives.

August 1st

Something to remember

Don't fret because of evildoers, neither be envious against those who work unrighteousness. [2] For they shall soon be cut down like the grass, and wither like the green herb.
(Psalm 37:1-2)

Today we're starting to go through the first 11 verses of Psalm 37. The psalmist starts by telling us not to fret or be anxious about non-believers who do wrong, and not to be envious of the way things seem to work out for them. Whatever happens to them in this life, they will spend eternity in torment if they don't turn to Jesus before they die. And we are on our way to heaven.

AUGUST 2ND

Something to determine

Trust in the LORD, and do good.
(Psalm 37:3)

This verse contrasts with the first two of yesterday. We belong to Jesus. Instead of wasting emotional energy on the unrighteous, let's put our focus on God and determine to trust Him. Instead of doing wrong like others do, let's do good. Helping others is a great antidote to anxiety and fear.

AUGUST 3RD

Something to enjoy

Dwell in the land, and enjoy safe pasture.
(Psalm 37:3)

We live in this world but we are not of it. Our true home is the Kingdom of God. This world is full of fear and negativity, but God's Kingdom is full of hope and light. As we live in relationship with God our Father, we are safe and have all our needs met. Let's not get bogged down in the cares and fears of this world. Let's live in our spiritual home even as we walk this earth.

August 4th

Something to take on board

Also delight yourself in the LORD, and he will give you the desires of your heart.

(Psalm 37:4)

The world is following its own desires but those desires don't lead to peace. They are much more likely to lead to fear and anxiety. Some people have everything they think they could possibly want, but so often we hear of the lives of the rich and famous falling apart. Don't desire what the world goes after. Take your pleasure in the Lord and He will put desires in your heart which are good and eternal and which lead to peace, not fear.

AUGUST 5TH

Something to put into practice

Commit your way to the LORD.
(Psalm 37:5)

When you have a decision to make, instead of tossing different scenarios around in your mind all the time and inviting fear in, ask God the way to go. And when you believe you have heard His direction, step out in it. He will show you if you've got it wrong. That's the way to peace.

AUGUST 6TH

Something to grasp

Trust also in him, and he will do this: [6] he will make your righteousness shine out like light, and your justice as the noon day sun.

(Psalm 37:5-6)

As we step out, trusting God to direct us, look what He does. He makes our righteousness, which Jesus has won for us, shine out like light. And as we make more right decisions and fewer wrong ones, our justice shines out to others as brightly as the sun at midday. Wow! That's quite something. It's so easy to live our lives feeling insignificant and fearful of how others see us. Trust in God and He will make you shine. Thank You Lord!

August 7th

Something to put into practice

Rest in the LORD, and wait patiently for him.
(Psalm 37:7)

It's so easy to get into mental and emotional turmoil when things are difficult. The world will offer all sorts of ideas to try and give us peace. Some may work for a while, but there is only one place to go to find real peace which you can rest in, and which will always be there for you. And that's the Lord.

The psalmist tells us to rest in Him. Don't waste time and effort following other paths. Go to the Lord in His Word and you can find true rest for your soul – all your thoughts and emotions. It takes determination to stay focused on God and cast down negative thoughts, but keep going, waiting patiently, and the end result will truly satisfy. Rest in Him and Him alone.

AUGUST 8TH

Something else to put into practice

Don't fret because of him who prospers in his way, because of the man who makes wicked plots happen. [8] Cease from anger, and forsake wrath. Don't fret; it leads only to evildoing.

(Psalm 37:7-8)

This verse is very similar to verse 1. We know there are people who have great wealth and fame which they have acquired through unlawful or immoral means. God tells us not to fret about it. He warns us that if we worry about it, we put ourselves in the way of temptation to copy them and do wrong ourselves. That can only lead to trouble and trouble leads to fear. Choose God's way and find rest.

AUGUST 9TH

Something to remember

For evildoers shall be cut off, but those who wait for the LORD shall inherit the land. [10] For yet a little while, and the wicked will be no more. Yes, though you look for his place, he isn't there. [11] But the humble shall inherit the land, and shall delight themselves in the abundance of peace.

(Psalm 37:9-11)

Today we come to the last verses in the section of Psalm 37 we are looking at. They explain what will ultimately happen to those who do evil in the sight of the Lord. They will be cut off from heaven. They will be spending eternity in hell if they don't accept Jesus before they die.

But we who are born-again inherit God's Kingdom in this life and for eternity. Because of Jesus, we can delight in peace no matter what is going on around us. And not just peace, but an abundance of peace – fear cannot stand in the face of that! Trust God; He will sort everything out one day according to His perfect justice.

AUGUST 10TH

Something to rejoice about

For you are all children of God, through faith in Christ Jesus.

(Galatians 3:26)

I've included this verse to remind us again that it is through faith in Jesus that we became children of God. It wasn't by our own effort, by being good or going to church or reading our Bible or praying. We could never do enough good things to earn our way to heaven. It is only by believing that Jesus suffered the punishment for all our sin and accepting Him as our Lord and Saviour, that we become children of God.

If you ever get fearful about whether you are God's child, don't look at what you've done, either good to affirm you or bad to condemn you. Instead, look at what Jesus has done and rejoice that, because of Him, you are indeed a child of God.

AUGUST 11TH

Something to hold onto

Who shall separate us from the love of Christ? Could oppression, or anguish, or persecution, or famine, or nakedness, or peril, or sword? 36 Even as it is written, "For your sake we are killed all day long. We were accounted as sheep for the slaughter." 37 No, in all these things we are more than conquerors through him who loved us.
(Romans 8:35-37)

There are terrible things happening in the world and Christians are suffering persecution all the time. When you are hurting or you hear of others suffering for their faith, it is easy to let fear in and ask the question, "Does God really love me?" or "Does God really love them?" Don't listen to the lies of the devil. The answer is always "Yes."

Jesus underwent the worse persecution that anyone has ever suffered or will ever suffer. If He wasn't saved from persecution, then neither are we. But hold on to this promise – whatever is done to us or to others, nothing can separate us from God's love. And because He has conquered death by coming back from the dead, we are conquerors too. Silence fear by declaring to yourself that nothing, absolutely nothing, can ever separate you from God's love.

AUGUST 12TH

Something to know

Jesus Christ is the same yesterday, today, and forever.
(Hebrews 13:8)

The world may be in turmoil and fear may be everywhere, but Jesus remains the same as He always has been, as He is today and as He always will be. All that He has done and won for us still stands and always will stand.

People may reject Him but He remains the same. People may insult Him but He remains the same. People may deny Him but He remains the same. People may mock Him but He remains the same. He is the Son of God, our Lord and Saviour. Hold onto the one sure foundation for your life and fear will be silenced.

August 13th

Something to declare

I will meditate on your precepts, and consider your ways. [16] I will delight myself in your statutes. I will not forget your word.

(Psalm 119:15-16)

Once again the psalmist tells us to read God's Word, meditate on it, think about what it means and delight in it. When things are going well, don't forget God's Word. When things are going badly don't forget God's Word. Keep it in the front of your mind and it will be there ready for you, so the Holy Spirit can remind you of what you need to hear in any situation. Don't listen to the voice of fear – listen to the voice of God in His Word, and you will be able to walk forward confidently, trusting in Him.

August 14th

Something to determine

The Lord said, "If you had faith like a grain of mustard seed, you would tell this sycamore tree, 'Be uprooted and be planted in the sea,' and it would obey you."
(Luke 17:6)

Jesus had told His disciples that if they had faith as small as a mustard seed, they would be able to command the mountains to go into the sea. Here He says that with a small amount of faith they could tell a huge tree to be uprooted and be planted in the sea and it would. So what does He mean by mountains and trees?

They represent the big problems that we face in life – the things that stand in our way looking so big there seems no way round them or over them; the things that stand in our way which are so firmly rooted that it doesn't seem possible to dig them out; the things that stand in our way that fill us with fear. Jesus says all we need is faith, not cancelled out by doubt or unbelief or fear.

Let's determine again to root out unbelief. Let's take Jesus at His Word and command the mountains and trees in our lives to move in His name. Let's stand in faith until they go. Thank You Lord.

AUGUST 15TH

Something to determine

Jesus said to him, "Because you have seen me, you have believed. Blessed are those who have not seen and have believed."

(John 20:29)

The first time Jesus appeared to His disciples after He had come back from the dead, they were all together except for Thomas. What a time to be missing! When the others told him what had happened, Thomas refused to believe it had been Jesus. He said he wanted physical proof by seeing and touching the wounds Jesus had suffered on the Cross.

What was he thinking? Was he afraid of believing something that hadn't been proved to him? Jesus came again when Thomas was there and invited him to touch His wounds. But once Thomas saw Him, he didn't need to – he knew it was Jesus and that Jesus was indeed Lord and God.

Jesus then said the words in today's verse. Those who have not seen and have believed are us. Thomas wasn't as blessed as he might have been, because he had doubted. We can't see Jesus physically, so we have no choice but to believe in Him by faith. Don't get caught up in trying to prove everything about Jesus and who He is – that's doubt and will lead to fear, not blessing. Choose to use your faith and believe – fear will be silenced and you will be blessed.

AUGUST 16TH

Something to determine

"You shall not be afraid of the face of man, for the judgement is God's."

(Deuteronomy 1:17)

We've had quite a few verses like this one. It's something we really need to remember when people come against us. Determine not to be afraid of them – God's justice will prevail in the next life if not in this one.

AUGUST 17TH

<u>Something to declare</u>

But thanks be to God, who gives us the victory through our Lord Jesus Christ.

(1 Corinthians 15:57)

Jesus has won the complete victory over anything and everything that would try to come against you and fill you with fear. He won it for you so, as you stand with Him, it becomes your victory. Declare this verse out loud and praise God. Persevere and fear will go. Thanks be to God!

AUGUST 18TH

Something to act upon

"You shall not forget the covenant that I have made with you. You shall not fear other gods. [39] But you shall fear the LORD your God, and he will deliver you out of the hand of all your enemies."

(2 Kings 17:38-39)

The word translated 'fear' in this verse doesn't mean to be afraid; it means to respect and hold in awe. Let's ask ourselves the question – do we fear any other gods? Our immediate answer is probably no. But take a moment to think about the things and people who are important in your life. Here's a few ideas to help you – how about football or other sport, your job, holidays, the news, TV, money, celebrities, social media, video games, music, even family, and you add more. I'm not saying it's always wrong to enjoy these things, but they need to be in the right place in our lives. We can become obsessed by them and even addicted. If they are too important, then they become other gods and will take the place of God.

God Himself is the only One who is worthy of our awe and respect. Put Him first and seek His ways. Live in relationship with Him and He will help you and protect you as no other thing or person can. Only He is the answer to your fears. Only He can bring you peace and lasting joy.

AUGUST 19TH

Something to put into practice

Whoever guards his mouth and his tongue keeps his soul from troubles.
(Proverbs 21:23)

Again the Bible reminds us to be careful about what we say. Our tongues can get us into a lot of trouble. And trouble leads to fear. Ask the Lord to help you be alert to what you're just about to say. You then have a split second to decide whether it's for good or not. The more you guard your tongue, the easier it will become to do so and the fewer troubles will come your way.

AUGUST 20TH

Something to base your life on

Be subject therefore to God. Resist the devil, and he will flee from you.

(James 4:7)

This is a brilliant verse to live by. We need to apply it to our thoughts before they become words or actions. Remember, Jesus tells us in John 10:10 that good is from God and bad is from the devil. Good brings peace and bad brings fear. Choose to be subject to God and what He is doing – go with it, follow it and give it priority in your life. And resist the devil and all his schemes – say, "No! I know who you are and what you are trying to do. I'm not listening. I'm a child of God. I resist you in the name of Jesus and you have to flee."

Keep at it. Follow God and peace, and resist the devil and fear. You will see – he will flee. Hallelujah!

AUGUST 21ST

Something to remember

Remember this: he who sows sparingly will also reap sparingly. He who sows bountifully will also reap bountifully.

(2 Corinthians 9:6)

This verse comes in a passage about money and giving. But I believe it is a principle that can be applied in all walks of life.

Are you fearful because you're struggling in some way? It may be financially or it may be in relationships with others, in your job, in your family. It is good to take our eyes off what we are going through and focus on the other person or people involved in the situation. How can we help them? How can we bless them? How can we make their life better? Sow good into difficult situations and you will reap good. Sow it generously and you will reap generously.

Fear always focuses us on ourselves. So when it tries to limit you, pull the rug from under its feet by focusing on others. As you bless them, fear will be silenced and you will indeed reap bountifully. Thank You Lord!

AUGUST 22ND

Something to take hold of

For in Christ Jesus neither is circumcision anything, nor uncircumcision, but a new creation. [16] As many as walk by this rule, peace and mercy be on them, and on God's Israel.
(Galatians 6:15-16)

God established the practice of circumcision with Abraham who was to be the father of the Jewish people. A thousand years later, when God led His people into the land which He had promised them, He gave them the law and incorporated circumcision into it.

But when Jesus came and died for us, taking the punishment for all our failures and sins, the law was no longer relevant. What matters now, isn't that we keep the law, but that we accept Jesus as our Lord and Saviour. It is then that are we are given a brand-new, perfect spirit, the Holy Spirit comes to live in us and we become a new creation.

Trying to please God by following rules and traditions and going through rituals just leads down the road of striving and failure, and that leads to the fear of God's rejection. But living our lives in the knowledge that He has made us new and there is nothing we can do to make Him love us more and nothing we can do to make Him love us less, is the way to peace. That is the rule to follow. It is through God's mercy that we can walk away from fear and know His peace.

August 23rd

Something to act upon

Get wisdom. Get understanding. Don't forget, and don't deviate from the words of my mouth. [6] Don't forsake her, and she will preserve you. Love her, and she will keep you.
(Proverbs 4:5-6)

So many times in the Bible God reminds us to get to know His Word and let it guide us and direct us in every area of our lives. His Word has power to keep us safe when we stand upon it in faith. So instead of listening to the voice of fear, let's go to the Word of God. Decide today that His Word is the truth and has the answer to all our questions and all our needs.

Let's get it, not forget it, keep to it, never move away from it and love it. It will preserve us and keep us.

AUGUST 24TH

Something to take on board

For who is God, except the LORD? Who is a rock, besides our God, [32] the God who arms me with strength, and makes my way perfect?

(Psalm 18:31-32)

You can believe what you want, but it will benefit you nothing if it isn't true. Only the Lord God is God. He is the only One you can build your life on as a rock-solid foundation. He's the only One who will give you strength and lead you in His perfect plan for your life.

Don't get caught up in other ways which will only end up in fear. Stick with God – the One and only, and He will direct you on the best possible plan for your life and give you peace.

August 25th

Something to put into practice

Jesus spoke to them, saying, "I am the light of the world. He who follows me will not walk in the darkness, but will have the light of life."
(John 8:12)

Earlier we read that God is the light of the world. In this verse Jesus tells us that He is the light of the world. There is no contradiction here because Jesus is God Himself.

If you are walking along a dark road it is difficult, if not impossible, to see where to put your feet. It is easy to feel afraid. However, if someone goes ahead of you with a light, you can then see the road and can confidently follow them. But if you went off to the right or the left, you would go beyond the reach of the light and would be back in the dark.

Jesus is light and shines everywhere He goes. If we follow Him, He will light our way and we can walk confidently along on the path He leads us on. But if we stray off the path, we will no longer be able to see His light and will open ourselves to fear. Let the light of Jesus lead you in every area of your life and, instead of the darkness of fear, you will have the light of life.

AUGUST 26TH

Something to remember

Then I said to you, "Don't be terrified. Don't be afraid of them. 30 The LORD your God, who goes before you, he will fight for you, according to all that he did for you in Egypt before your eyes, 31 and in the wilderness where you have seen how that the LORD your God carried you, as a man carries his son, in all the way that you went, until you came to this place."

(Deuteronomy 1:29-31)

Once again we have the words of Moses encouraging the Israelites before they entered the land God had promised them. They knew they would be facing battles and were understandably terrified. Moses helps them to overcome their fear by reminding them of how God had led them out of Egypt and through the desert to where they were now.

If you're feeling terrified because of a battle you're facing, take time to remember how God has led you and helped you before and think of all the wonderful things He has done in your life. God is faithful – what He's done before He will do again and new things too. Take courage and silence fear with thanks to Him for all He has done and will do.

AUGUST 27TH

Something to take hold of

When the enemy shall come in like a flood, the Spirit of the LORD shall lift up a standard against him.
(Isaiah 59:19 KJV)

I've quoted this verse from the King James Bible as it states this truth very clearly. When the devil is trying to beat you down, God raises up His standard for you to fight under. When you stand under His flag or banner, you are fighting on the side that has already won. The enemy is already defeated. There is no fear when God is on your side and you stand with Him.

August 28th

Something to determine

Trust in the LORD with all your heart, and don't lean on your own understanding. [6] In all your ways acknowledge him, and he will make your paths straight.

(Proverbs 3:5-6)

How often do we try and work things out for ourselves? How much time do we waste worrying and tossing things around in our minds? It never gives us peace. It just leaves us feeling exhausted and fearful.

Let's determine not to lean on our own understanding. Let's trust God instead. Go to His Word, pray and wait in faith, knowing that He will give you His wisdom.

And as you follow His leading, don't pretend to yourself or others that it was all your idea. Thank Him for showing you what to do. Then you will find that the way ahead is straight, rather than steep and crooked, and you will have peace, not fear.

August 29th

Something to obey

But the LORD said to me, "Don't say, 'I am a child;' for you must go to whomever I send you, and you must say whatever I command you. 8 Don't be afraid because of them, for I am with you to rescue you," says the LORD.
(Jeremiah 1:7-8)

Jeremiah was a prophet in the Old Testament, speaking God's words to His people. He was a young man when God called him to do this and felt inadequate and fearful, so he made the excuse that he was too young for the job. These verses are God's reply.

When God calls you to do something that makes you feel inadequate and afraid, don't make excuses. And don't talk negatively about it – remember, what you say has power. God will be with you and He will rescue you from difficult situations. So refuse to fear what other people may say or do. Just get on with what God has asked you to do, putting all your trust in Him.

AUGUST 30TH

Something to put into practice

Cast your burden on the LORD and he will sustain you. He will never allow the righteous to be moved.

(Psalm 55:22)

This is such a lovely picture. God is standing before you asking you to put all your burdens on Him. He's there waiting with His arms outstretched to receive them. But He won't take them from you – you have to hand them over. He will always respect your free will.

Why would we carry burdens that wear us down and make us fearful when God wants to carry them for us! Enough is enough. Start to hand them over and don't take them back. It's not easy, but the more we do it, the easier it becomes. Thank You Lord for carrying my burdens for me, for giving me all the energy and strength I need and for keeping me safe with You.

August 31st

Something to delight in

Now you are the body of Christ, and members individually.
(1 Corinthians 12:27)

The Christian church is the body of Christ on this earth. Jesus calls His church His bride – such a wonderful picture of our relationship with Him as our bridegroom. But He also sees us individually. Just as He sees a forest and also knows each individual tree, so it is with His church. Each one of us is unique and so special to Him.

Don't compare yourself with other Christians. Look to your bridegroom and receive His unconditional love just for you. Jesus would have died for you if you were the only person alive – that's how much He loves you. Silence fear of inadequacy or unworthiness with the truth of His infinite love for you. Delight in being part of the body of Christ and a member individually. Jesus delights in you.

September 1st

Something to take hold of

In the past, you were not a people, but now are God's people, who had not obtained mercy, but now have obtained mercy.

(1 Peter 2:10)

When there is the possibility of punishment there is fear. We all deserve punishment but instead of getting what we deserve we get what we don't deserve – God's mercy. It was shown to us as Jesus took our punishment so we could be free. God didn't say sin doesn't matter – He knew it had to be punished but He didn't want to punish us because He loves us so much. So He punished His own Son in our place so we could have mercy and be forgiven. And where there is mercy and forgiveness, fear has no place.

SEPTEMBER 2ND

Something to declare

"Behold, God is my salvation. I will trust, and will not be afraid; for the LORD, the LORD, is my strength and song; and he has become my salvation."
(Isaiah 12:2)

Isaiah was another of God's prophets in the Old Testament. He had made a decision not to be afraid, but to trust God – after all He was the One who had saved Him. So he declared aloud His trust in God and all that He was to Him.

Make this your declaration today – your faith will rise and the fear about what you're dealing with will disappear.

September 3rd

Something to realise

For as he thinketh in his heart, so is he.
(Proverbs 23:7 KJV)

Fear is a reaction to something that has happened or you imagine might happen. It's an emotional response, but it comes not so much from what is going on, as from how you react to it. The same thing could happen to two different people and one think positively about it and not be disturbed, while another think negatively and spiral down into fear. What they think determines how they are.

We really need to realise the truth of this. It's much easier to deal with fear before it takes root. The moment you start to feel fear, take control of the thoughts and cast them down. Replace them with the promises of God to give you wisdom and help you and lead you through. It's what He wants to do. Thank You Lord.

September 4th

Something to rejoice about

Summoning the apostles, they beat them and commanded them not to speak in the name of Jesus, and let them go. [41] They therefore departed from the presence of the council, rejoicing that they were counted worthy to suffer dishonour for Jesus' name. [42] Every day, in the temple and at home, they never stopped teaching and preaching Jesus, the Christ.

(Acts 5:40-42)

The disciples had been arrested and beaten for telling people about Jesus. How did they respond? They rejoiced that they were counted worthy to suffer for their faith in Jesus. Wow – that's some response.

If you find yourself being persecuted, know that how you respond is up to you. Choose not to focus on the anger and fear which can so easily get hold of you. Instead, start to rejoice that you are counted worthy to suffer as Jesus Himself did. I remember a time this happened to me. I took these verses and determined to follow the disciples' example. As I started to rejoice, I very quickly felt my faith rise, and hurt and fear were silenced. I then had to determine not to go back into my initial negative reaction.

When you deny fear the place it wants in your mind and your heart, you are free to continue to do what God wants you to do. Fear would have crippled the disciples' ministry, but rejoicing in Jesus enabled them to keep on telling others the good news of the Gospel.

September 5th

Something to put into practice

But if one of you suffers for being a Christian, let him not be ashamed; but let him glorify God in this matter.
(1 Peter 4:16)

Here is another verse about glorifying God when you suffer for your faith, instead of getting into negative emotions. Decide this will be your response now, before it is needed. I say again, you prepare for battle in times of peace.

SEPTEMBER 6TH

Something to take hold of

The LORD will make you the head, and not the tail. You will be above only, and you will not be beneath, if you listen to the commandments of the LORD your God which I command you today, to observe and to do, [14] and shall not turn away from any of the words which I command you today, to the right hand or to the left, to go after other gods to serve them.

(Deuteronomy 28:13-14)

This is a verse I have stood on in the past when things have threatened to overwhelm me. It's another of my favourite passages of Scripture. Moses spoke this when he gave the law to the Israelites. We are not under law, but under grace, so we replace the word 'commandments' with 'God's Word'. When we base our lives on the truth of God and all Jesus has done and won for us, then we can take hold of this wonderful promise.

You won't be the tail, dragged around after the body with no choice about where you go or what you do. No – God will make you the head. You will be the one able to determine where you go and what you do. You will be on top of the situations you find yourself in, not crushed underneath them. Hallelujah!

September 7th

Something to reassure you

No temptation has taken you except what is common to man. God is faithful, who will not allow you to be tempted above what you are able, but will with the temptation also make the way of escape, that you may be able to endure it.
(1 Corinthians 10:13)

When something difficult happens or threatens to happen it's very easy to give in to the temptation to fear. It's an age-old ploy of the devil to try to get you off God's perfect plan for your life and rock your faith. Whatever temptation he puts your way, know that it is never unique to you. The devil doesn't have any new ways to tempt; he just keeps using the same old ones he's used before. Never think that no-one else has had to deal with what you're dealing with.

God knows exactly what is going on and He will always give you the ability to say no to any temptation, including to fear. Jesus has already won the victory over the devil and all his schemes through the Cross. Thank You Lord that I can always resist the temptation to fear, and walk free in You.

September 8th

Something to remember

You are of God, little children, and have overcome them, because greater is he who is in you than he who is in the world.

(1 John 4:4)

Jesus has defeated the devil and all His schemes. As you stand with Him you have overcome them too. Remember, Jesus living in you is infinitely greater than the devil out there in the world. Overcomers have no need to fear and you are an overcomer. Thank You Jesus.

September 9th

Something to understand

For there is no partiality with God.
(Romans 2:11)

God has never discriminated against anyone because of their sex, race, age or anything else. If you are struggling in this area, for whatever reason, turn away from fear and praise God that He sees you as His child, born-again through Jesus. He has no other label for you. You are simply His.

SEPTEMBER 10TH

<u>Something to grasp</u>

There is neither Jew nor Greek, there is neither slave nor free man, there is neither male nor female; for you are all one in Christ Jesus.

(Galatians 3:28)

This verse emphasises yesterday's. Let this truth sink in. God sees all born-again Christians simply as His. He does not discriminate between us in any way. We are all one in Him.

September 11th

Something to take on board

And God is able to make all grace abound to you, that you, always having all sufficiency in everything, may abound to every good work.

(2 Corinthians 9:8)

God doesn't want you struggling in poverty. Why would any good father want that for His children? God has promised to supply all your needs (Philippians 4:19). Believe His promises and focus on Him, not on anxiety. Not only is He able to give you all you need, but much more as well, so that you can help others too.

September 12th

Something to understand

As for God, his way is perfect. The LORD's word is tried. He is a shield to all those who take refuge in him.

(Psalm 18:30)

The world isn't perfect. God gave us all free will and we live with the consequences of our choices individually, nationally and globally. But God's plans are perfect. Find His truth in His Word and set your compass to follow it. When things are difficult in this imperfect world and fear is threatening to overwhelm you, run to Him. He will protect you when you live in relationship with Him and trust Him.

September 13th

Something to take hold of

For if we have become united with him in the likeness of his death, we will also be part of his resurrection;
[6] knowing this, that our old man was crucified with him, that the body of sin might be done away with, so that we would no longer be in bondage to sin. [7] For he who has died has been freed from sin.

(Romans 6:5-7)

Do you remember how your old self was put to death with Jesus on the Cross and how, because of this, you are no longer held by sin – now you are able to say "No."

Do you worry when you get things wrong? Do you still fear God's judgement? Take hold of this truth; it is really important. You will still get things wrong, but you are set free from sin. It cannot dictate to you anymore. You are free to refuse it. And if you do sin, you are free to receive the forgiveness Jesus has already won for you on the Cross.

Don't focus on the fear of failing. Thank Jesus that He has won your forgiveness and one day you will be raised to life for eternity with Him. Thank you Jesus!

SEPTEMBER 14TH

<u>Something to take on board</u>

I have taught you in the way of wisdom. I have led you in straight paths. [12] When you go, your steps will not be hampered. When you run, you will not stumble.
(Proverbs 4:11-12)

The Bible teaches us God's wisdom. But have we taken it on board? Have we allowed it to direct the way we live? Do we follow its truth as we walk though life? These are questions it's good to ask ourselves from time to time. When we go the way of the world or just our own way, we find there are lots of opportunities for anxiety and fear.

Fear will make us stumble. It's hard to think straight when we are anxious. It's hard to make clear decisions when we are fearful. We've been taught true wisdom from God's Word, so let's learn it. Let's make it the basis for our decisions and we will find that our path through life will be easier and we will be able to run and not stumble.

September 15th

Something to determine

While he still spoke, one from the ruler of the synagogue's house came, saying to him, "Your daughter is dead. Don't trouble the Teacher." 50 But Jesus hearing it, answered him, "Don't be afraid. Only believe, and she will be healed."

(Luke 8:49-50)

Jairus had a daughter who was seriously ill. He heard that Jesus was in the area, so he went to find Him and asked Him to come and heal her. But while he was talking to Jesus someone came from his house with the news that his daughter had died, so there was no point in Jesus coming.

Believing for healing is one thing, but believing for someone to come back from the dead feels much more difficult. Fear must have entered Jairus's mind and his heart. He was responding by how he felt, not with the truth of who Jesus is. Jesus reassured him, telling him to not be afraid, but to believe and his daughter would be healed. Jesus went to Jairus's house and made all the mourners leave. He got rid of the atmosphere of unbelief. And then he raised the girl back to life.

When everything has gone wrong, don't focus on fear and unbelief. Get rid of it and determine to focus on all Jesus has done and won for you and on all the promises of God. Determine to believe against all the evidence in front of you, and you will see the victory just as Jairus did. Hallelujah!

SEPTEMBER 16TH

Something to take on board

"I have said these things to you while still living with you. 26 But the Counsellor, the Holy Spirit, whom the Father will send in my name, will teach you all things, and will remind you of all that I said to you."

(John 14:25-26)

After Jesus had gone back to heaven, God sent His Holy Spirit to live in all true believers. Jesus had explained this to His disciples, telling them that one of the things the Holy Spirit would do to help them, was to remind them of all He had said to them.

We have God's Word. When you find yourself in a difficult situation, the Holy Spirit will remind you of what God's Word says. And that word will help you to know what to do and how to do it.

But notice that the Holy Spirit will remind you, not tell you. To be reminded of something, you have to know it in the first place. So let's get to know God's Word more and more. Let's think about it and let it settle in our hearts. Then, when we need a specific word, the Holy Spirit can remind us of it and we can act upon it. If you will let it, God's Word will silence fear and lead us through and out of the other side of whatever we are facing.

SEPTEMBER 17TH

Something to encourage

For we are God's fellow workers.
(1 Corinthians 3:9)

Think about this. What a job description. You aren't just working for God – you are working with Him. The Free Dictionary defines 'fellow worker' as a 'person who joins with others in some activity or endeavour'. That's us. We're not struggling on trying our best, worrying about how things are going or not going. We are working with God in the things He wants us to do. That's quite something! Why would we fear when God works alongside us and we are working alongside Him!

SEPTEMBER 18TH

Something to understand

When the servant of the man of God had risen early and gone out, behold, an army with horses and chariots was around the city. His servant said to him, "Alas, my master! What shall we do?" [16] He answered, "Don't be afraid, for those who are with us are more than those who are with them." [17] Elisha prayed, and said, "LORD, please open his eyes, that he may see." the LORD opened the young man's eyes, and he saw; and behold, the mountain was full of horses and chariots of fire around Elisha.

(2 Kings 6:15-17)

Syria was making war against Israel. The king of Syria had learned that the king of Israel would be in Dothan, so he sent his armies by night to surround the city, ready to take it in the daylight. When the people of the city woke up in the morning, they saw that they were surrounded by an army of soldiers with horses and chariots.

The prophet Elisha was there with his servant. The servant was filled with fear and asked Elisha what they should do. Elisha didn't try to reassure him with glib words. He asked God to show his servant the truth of what was really going on. God answered his prayer and the servant saw God's supernatural army surrounding them which was far greater and mightier than that of the Syrians.

You may be facing a battle where everything seems to be ranged against you and you are filled with fear. Remember, God is on your side and His army is far greater than any earthly one. Ask God to open your eyes to His power and might. Put all your trust in Him and you will see the victory.

September 19th

Something to reassure you

Thou wilt keep him in perfect peace, whose mind is stayed on thee: because he trusteth in thee.

(Isaiah 26:3 KJV)

Fear and peace cannot exist in the same place. Keep your focus on God and trust Him, and you have this promise to stand on – He will keep you in perfect peace.

September 20th

Something to decide

But God commends his own love towards us, in that while we were yet sinners, Christ died for us. [9] Much more then, being now justified by his blood, we will be saved from God's wrath through him. [10] For if while we were enemies, we were reconciled to God through the death of his Son, much more, being reconciled, we will be saved by his life.
(Romans 5:8-10)

Many people believe that God is angry with them. They think that they'll only go to heaven if they've been good. Have I done enough to get into heaven? Will God be cross with me? Is He going to send me to hell? There's so much fear behind these questions. God does hate sin but He loves people. He loved us even before we accepted Jesus. He loved us so much that He sent Jesus to die for us while we were still sinners. He didn't wait for us to get our act together. Jesus then came back from the dead to confirm everything He had achieved on the Cross, winning our complete salvation.

The result is that we are saved from God's anger forever. Yes, He still hates sin, but Jesus took the punishment for it all, completely satisfying God's anger. Decide to believe what the Bible tells you instead of listening to your own fearful thoughts and the lies of the devil. God looks on you with nothing but love, and perfect love casts out fear.

September 21st

<u>Something to realise</u>

For the thing which I fear comes on me, that which I am afraid of comes to me.

(Job 3:25)

This is Job speaking after he had lost everything. He realises that he had been afraid this would happen. What we think about eventually comes out of our mouths and we have seen how powerful words are. Don’t waste mental and emotional energy imagining the worst. Think of God's truth in Jesus and all His wonderful promises and they will be what you speak about. Don’t let fear control your life. Let Jesus have His way instead.

September 22nd

Something to act upon

Humble yourselves therefore under the mighty hand of God, that he may exalt you in due time ...
(1 Peter 5:6)

To do this, we need to first understand what 'humble' means in the Bible. It doesn't mean being a doormat for others to walk on. It doesn't mean running yourself down all the time. It doesn't mean having low self-esteem. It means not having an inflated opinion of yourself; not considering yourself better than others; not putting yourself in the place of God. Being truly humble under God brings peace – there is no striving in it or fear of failure.

This verse tells us to humble ourselves, so this is something that is not only possible for us to do, but which is good for us to do. Don't run yourself down, but don't put yourself above others or God either. The opposite to being humble is being proud. Our world doesn't think being humble is good. It encourages us to take pride in who we are and what we've done. But God hates pride and loves humility.

Don't push yourself forward all the time or insist on your rights – it will only lead to anger, fear and frustration. Be humble and you will find that God exalts you at the right time. When that happens, give Him the glory and continue living your life in humility before Him.

SEPTEMBER 23RD

Something to put into practice

... casting all your worries on him, because he cares for you.
(1 Peter 5:7)

It's really interesting that casting our worries on God is part of the same sentence that we looked at yesterday about humbling ourselves. What's the connection? If we decide that we're going to do everything our own way and solve all our problems by ourselves, not accepting help from anyone else including God, that's the opposite of being humble – it's pride.

God cares for you so much; He longs to take your worries and fears from you and lead you through what you're facing in victory, not defeat. How do we cast all our cares on Him and not take them back? I think that last bit is the most difficult – not taking them back or, in other words, not carrying on worrying about them.

Years ago someone told me to imagine a bin with a loose lid which was standing at the foot of the Cross. In my imagination, I was to put the things that bothered me in the bin and put the lid on. I could put my cares in the bin, but I found it difficult to put the lid on. When I eventually did put it on, I kept wanting to lift it a little and peep inside. I had to discipline myself to leave it alone.

The bin is at the foot of the Cross, because it was there that Jesus won the victory over anything and everything that would try to come against us – every care, every worry, every fear. So what is the point in carrying them ourselves. Let's humble ourselves and continually cast our worries on God and leave them there, because He cares for us.

SEPTEMBER 24TH

Something to understand

Let no man say when he is tempted, "I am tempted by God," for God can't be tempted by evil, and he himself tempts no one. [14] But each one is tempted when he is drawn away by his own lust and enticed. [15] Then the lust, when it has conceived, bears sin. The sin, when it is full grown, produces death.

(James 1:13-15)

When you feel the temptation to think, say or do something wrong, never justify giving in to it by saying that it's God who is tempting you. God will never, never tempt you to sin. It's the devil who puts the temptation in your way, and it's you that gives in to it. Sin never has a good end. Ultimately it leads to death. But this is not to condemn you or make you fearful – the opposite. No-one lives a perfect life, but Jesus has suffered all the punishment we deserve and when we are born-again God's forgiveness is there for us to freely receive.

Don't be afraid of temptation. God will always give you the strength to say "No" to it. Instead, rejoice in your forgiveness and be thankful.

SEPTEMBER 25TH

Something to put into practice

"Don't let your heart be troubled. Believe in God. Believe also in me."

(John 14:1)

These were the first words Jesus said to His disciples following the Last Supper. It was the night they were going to see Him arrested and the day before He would be crucified. Their whole world was about to collapse dramatically and He told them not to let their heart be troubled.

What does it mean to have a troubled heart? We probably have all experienced what it is like to some degree or another. It's a horrible feeling – it is having your thoughts and emotions full of fear and anxiety and imagining all sorts of negative possibilities.

But Jesus told them and tells us not to let our hearts be troubled. In other words, it's under our control and we can stop it from happening. I know there will be people who will adamantly deny that, but if Jesus says it, then it's true. So the question is – how do we do it?

Jesus said to believe in God and believe in Him. Lots of people believe God exists, but not so many have accepted Jesus as their Lord and Saviour. Be born-again, focus on God, speak His word out, think about all Jesus has done and won for you. Keep at it and you will find you can indeed conquer fear and not let your heart be troubled.

September 26th

Something to take hold of

When I saw him, I fell at his feet like a dead man. He laid his right hand on me, saying, "Don't be afraid. I am the first and the last, [18] and the Living one. I was dead, and behold, I am alive forever and ever. Amen."

(Revelation 1:17-18)

This was part of a vision the apostle John had after Jesus had gone back to heaven. He had spent three years with Jesus on earth, but now He saw Him in all His glory and He fell at His feet in awe. Jesus still had the same attitude towards John. He showed His love and care as He told him not to be afraid. He assured John that He was the same Jesus come back from the dead and alive for evermore.

This is so important for us to take hold of. We don't serve a dead man, but a living Saviour – the One who always has been and always will be. Mediate on this and let it still your anxious thoughts and silence fear.

September 27th

Something to take on board

For through him we both have our access in one Spirit to the Father.

(Ephesians 2:18)

When we were born-again, the Holy Spirit merged with our brand-new perfect spirit making us one with Jesus. So through Him we can live in close relationship with God – He as our Father and us as His children.

Do you worry sometimes that you can't approach God; that you aren't worthy? Silence those thoughts with this truth. You are one with Jesus and therefore you always have access to God. No discussion. Thank You Lord.

September 28th

Something to grasp

For sin will not have dominion over you, for you are not under law, but under grace.
(Romans 6:14)

Once again we read that we are free from being held captive by sin. The people who lived under the law in the Old Testament had to try to obey the rules and this made them very aware of their sin. But our sin has been punished in Jesus and the record of all our sin has been done away with. That's grace.

Under the law we get what we deserve – punishment with its condemnation and fear. But under grace we get what we don't deserve – mercy, forgiveness, new life, the love and blessings of God showered upon us in this life, and eternity with Jesus.

Which would you choose? If you aren't born-again, go back to January 5th and make today the day you step from captivity into freedom, from fear into peace, from law into grace.

If you are born-again, take a moment to look at your attitude to God. Even though you're free from the law, are you still trying to earn your way into His favour somehow? Turn your thoughts around and rejoice at the truth that sin no longer has dominion over you, for you are not under law, but under grace.

September 29th

Something to determine

Having therefore, brothers, boldness to enter into the holy place by the blood of Jesus, [20] by the way which he dedicated for us, a new and living way, through the veil, that is to say, his flesh, [21] and having a great priest over God's house, [22] let's draw near with a true heart in fullness of faith, having our hearts sprinkled from an evil conscience and having our body washed with pure water, [23] let's hold fast the confession of our hope without wavering; for he who promised is faithful.

(Hebrews 10:19-23)

Because we are free to be in relationship with God through Jesus's death and resurrection, let's do what this verse says and draw near to God boldly. We can do so confidently, not because of anything we've done, but because of what Jesus has done for us.

If you are fearful, you cannot be confident. If you are truly confident, then you have no fear. Determine not to waver in your faith in what Jesus has done for you in winning your forgiveness, washing you completely clean of sin and setting you free from its guilt and shame.

Fear be silenced. I belong to Jesus and I draw near to my Father God boldly. I refuse to waver in my faith, for God is faithful to His promises and I receive them all in Jesus. Amen.

September 30th

Something to take hold of

"I have come as a light into the world, that whoever believes in me may not remain in the darkness."
(John 12:46)

Jesus is the light of the world. If you believe in Him and all He has done and won for you, then your brand-new spirit is living in His light all the time. Notice that this verse says that you may not remain in darkness, it doesn't say you will not. The way into the light is open to you but it's up to you to step into it.

Are your thoughts and emotions still living in the darkness of fear and anxiety and worry? Renew them through the truth of God's Word and bring them into line with His truth already in your spirit, and you will indeed no longer remain in darkness, but live in the light of Jesus.

It's not an instant thing – it takes determination and practice and perseverance. But start to do it and you will gradually find that you are leaving the darkness of fear behind and living more and more in the light of Jesus. Praise Him!

October 1st

Something to realise

Put on the whole armour of God, that you may be able to stand against the wiles of the devil. [12] For our wrestling is not against flesh and blood, but against the principalities, against the powers, against the world's rulers of the darkness of this age, and against the spiritual forces of wickedness in the heavenly places.

(Ephesians 6:11-12)

We are going to spend the next eight days looking at the armour of God. It's good to meditate on it bit by bit each day, rather than always reading it all at once. Give it time to sink into your heart and impact how you approach your daily life.

We start with the reason God asks us to put on His armour. Its whole purpose is to protect us from the devil and his wiles or schemes, so we can stand strong in our faith. Wouldn't we all want that?

First, we have to remember that our battle is not against the people the devil may use to attack us, but against him. This is so important to remember when people come against us.

If people come against you and your faith, remember, your battle isn't with them, but with the devil who is using them to try and make you fearful and weaken your faith. But God has the answer.

OCTOBER 2ND

Something to reassure you

Therefore put on the whole armour of God, that you may be able to withstand in the evil day, and having done all, to stand.

(Ephesians 6:13)

Did yesterday's verses make you feel a bit fearful? Well, be reassured, no matter what the devil tries to throw at you, God has provided everything you need to stand against him and win the battle. Not only can you withstand the devil, but you are able to stand secure and confident in Jesus and the victory He has won for you.

Determine to live your life wearing all the armour of God and stand safe in Jesus.

OCTOBER 3RD

Something to put on

Stand therefore, having the utility belt of truth buckled around your waist ...

(Ephesians 6:14)

Today we start looking at the first of the six individual parts of God's armour – the belt of truth. A belt goes round your middle holding everything together.

A weightlifter wears a belt for various reasons. Here are three I have found. It stabilises the body and reduces stress on it; it helps the weightlifter to use the right muscles and not over flex the wrong ones; and it may help increase muscle power and sustain it.

Having got hold of the truth of God in His Word, we need to wear it around us. We need it all the time, but especially when we have a weight to lift – something that we face and have to deal with. God's truth will stabilise us and reduce stress. It will help us to know what to do and what not to do. And it will increase the power of Jesus in our lives and help us to sustain it. Three excellent reasons to wrap the truth of God around you. The result is that you will be better able to resist fear and stand firm in every situation that you face.

October 4th

Something to wear

... and having put on the breastplate of righteousness ...
(Ephesians 6:14)

Next is the breastplate of righteousness. When you know that you have been given a brand-new perfect spirit and made righteous in the sight of God, you are protected from the devil's lies trying to tell you that you are inadequate and God can't possibly love you. Refuse to give in to these emotions. Say out loud, "I know who you are and I'm not listening; I have been made righteous in Jesus and nothing can change that. Thank You Lord."

OCTOBER 5TH

Something to walk in

... and having fitted your feet with the preparation of the Good News of peace ...
(Ephesians 6:15)

Because Jesus suffered the punishment for all our sins, we are forgiven and God is not angry with us – in fact He is at peace with us. Peace with God is the very essence of the gospel or the Good News. We can fearlessly stand against the devil when we know for sure that we have peace with God.

When the devil whispers in your ear, reminding you of what you've done in the past, tell him you're not listening because you are at peace with God through Jesus. Hallelujah!

OCTOBER 6TH

Something to stand behind

... above all, taking up the shield of faith, with which you will be able to quench all the fiery darts of the evil one.
(Ephesians 6:16)

Base your faith on the truth in God's Word, and when the devil throws his fiery darts into your mind, hold your faith up; the fire of the darts will be put out and the darts themselves will fall harmlessly to the ground.

Speak your faith out in the face of attack and fear cannot overwhelm you – its power will be quenched and it will simply fall away. Thank You Jesus.

OCTOBER 7TH

Something to wear

And take the helmet of salvation ...
(Ephesians 6:17)

The last item of protective armour is the helmet of salvation. We have to know that we are saved. If you entertain doubt, you are opening the door to fear. Know that you know that you know that you are saved. Refuse to listen to any voice that would tell you otherwise. Speak the truth of all Jesus has done and won for you from God's Word and you will be safe.

October 8th

Something to use

… and the sword of the Spirit, which is the word of God.
(Ephesians 6:17)

And here we come to the last part of the armour and this is an offensive weapon – a sword. It isn't there just to protect you, but for you to actively fight with. You may think it would be better to have lots of weapons, but you only need one – the Word of God.

When the devil tries to come against you, strike him through with God's truth. He cannot stand against it. When fear threatens, speak out the Word of God and see fear fall to the ground dead.

Thank You Lord for all your armour. Please remind me to wear it and use it day by day in the sure knowledge that it will protect me and cause my enemies to flee. Thank You Jesus for providing it all. Amen.

OCTOBER 9TH

Something to obey

"You therefore put your belt on your waist, arise, and say to them all that I command you. Don't be dismayed at them."

(Jeremiah 1:17)

When people come against you, refuse to be dismayed or fearful; fasten the belt of truth around you and go forward with complete confidence in the Word of God.

OCTOBER 10TH

Something to determine

Therefore we don't faint, but though our outward person is decaying, yet our inward person is renewed day by day,
[17] For our light affliction, which is for the moment, works for us more and more exceedingly an eternal weight of glory,
[18] while we don't look at the things which are seen, but at the things which are not seen. For the things which are seen are temporal, but the things which are not seen are eternal.

(2 Corinthians 4:16-18)

God made us with five senses (sight, hearing, smell, taste and touch) which we need to use all the time to live and survive in this world. But, as born-again Christians, we also have spiritual ears and eyes which enable us to understand what is going on beyond the physical realm.

You may be going through a really difficult time, but don't focus on what you can see, hear, smell, taste and feel. Focus on what is waiting for you – glory beyond imagining. Making Jesus your focus will stop you from fainting with fear. All the suffering of this world will pass away, but living in glory with Jesus will last forever.

OCTOBER 11TH

Something to put into practice

"Don't remember the former things, and don't consider the things of old. [19] Behold, I will do a new thing. It springs out now. Don't you know it? I will even make a way in the wilderness, and rivers in the desert."
(Isaiah 43:18-19)

These are the words of God spoken through His prophet, Isaiah. God was telling His people that living under the law would come to an end, and that He would do a new thing by sending His Son Jesus to save them from their sins. The old time of the law would come to an end and the new time of grace would begin.

We live in the time of that 'new thing' now. As a believer in Jesus you are not under law, but under grace. So forget all your past failings and fears. God has done a new thing in you – choose to live in the freedom of His grace.

October 12th

Something to declare

I can do all things through Christ who strengthens me.
(Philippians 4:13)

What a great verse to declare out loud when you feel fearful of what is ahead. In any situation, seek what God wants you to do and know that you can indeed do it, when you cast fear down, refuse to doubt and put your faith in Jesus. Thank You Lord.

October 13th

Something to grasp

This is the boldness which we have towards him, that if we ask anything according to his will, he listens to us. [15] And if we know that he listens to us, whatever we ask, we know that we have the petitions which we have asked of him.
(1 John 5:14-15)

How often do you pray and don't seem to get an answer? Do you wonder if God has heard your prayer or why He hasn't answered? Do you fear that you're not good enough for God to hear you or answer you? Grasp the truth in these verses.

If you ask according to His will, He does hear you. In fact, He does more than just hear you, He listens to you. Wait in faith, believing this, and you can be sure that the answer will come.

So if you feel God isn't answering your prayer, don't look at God, wondering what He is doing or not doing. Look at yourself. Are you asking according to His will? And are you waiting for your answer in fear or in faith? God is always faithful.

OCTOBER 14TH

Something to understand

"Come now, and let's reason together," says the LORD: "Though your sins are as scarlet, they shall be as white as snow. Though they are red like crimson, they shall be as wool."

(Isaiah 1:18)

Being a Christian isn't primarily about having supernatural experiences and being on a high with God. It is about knowing the truth and letting that truth settle in your mind and in your heart. If you just go for spiritual highs without understanding what Jesus has done for you and how God worked your salvation through Him, then your faith will be on shaky ground. When the highs go away, what have you got to stand on? God said to His people, "Let's reason together." A few times in the book of Acts we are told that the apostle Paul reasoned with people when he shared the gospel with them.

Make sure you understand what your faith is built on, then, when problems come along you will not be prey to fear. You will then be able to declare the truth in the face of the problem and fear will not take hold. Let's use the brains God gave us to reason through our faith and then allow it to settle into our hearts and become a true part of who we really are in Jesus.

OCTOBER 15TH

Something to put into practice

Blessed be the God and Father of our Lord Jesus Christ, the Father of mercies and God of all comfort, [4] who comforts us in all our affliction, that we may be able to comfort those who are in any affliction, through the comfort with which we ourselves are comforted by God. [5] For as the sufferings of Christ abound to us, even so our comfort also abounds through Christ.

(2 Corinthians 1:3-5)

God is the God of all comfort (2 Corinthians 1:3) and Jesus called the Holy Spirit the Comforter (John 14:26). God does not see you suffer for Him and just sit back and watch. He longs to comfort you. Never doubt that His love and comfort abound towards you. You just have to receive it.

When things get difficult, go to His Word and read His words of love for you and promises of help and protection. Declare them out loud. Allow Him to comfort you and fear will be silenced. Then let's take our eyes off ourselves and seek to comfort others who are suffering, in the same way God has comforted us.

OCTOBER 16TH

Something to take hold of

Even the youths shall faint and be weary, and the young men shall utterly fall: [31] But they that wait upon the LORD shall renew their strength; they shall mount up with wings as eagles; they shall run, and not be weary; and they shall walk, and not faint.

(Isaiah 40:30-31 KJV)

It is possible for anyone, whatever their age and however strong they are, to succumb to weariness and despair and fear. But we don't have to give in to it. As children of God, we have this wonderful promise.

But what does it mean to wait upon the Lord? A waiter waits upon tables in a restaurant. He focuses on the people at his or her tables and serves them, responding to their requests. When we wait upon the Lord, we focus on Him, seeking to discern what He wants us to do and then doing it.

When things pile up upon us and we feel the tug of weariness and despair and fear, let's determine to turn our focus on to Jesus and seek Him and the plans He has for us. Then we shall indeed be able to rise up above our problems as eagles soar in the air. Once they are up in the air, they don't flap their wings like other birds; they soar on currents of air with little effort. Don't let's flap about near the ground using up all our physical, mental and emotional energy. Let's wait upon God and soar up in the air with Him – then we shall be able to live without getting weary and go where He directs us without fear. Thank You Lord.

October 17th

Something to act upon

But you, beloved, keep building up yourselves on your most holy faith, praying in the Holy Spirit.
(Jude 1:20)

This is such an important verse. What do you do when things get on top of you and you start to feel fearful? Jude tells us to build up our faith. Don't listen to your feelings – they won't build your faith because they will always vary, but the truth of God is constant and will build your faith. And don't ask God to give you more faith. He's given you all the faith you will ever need. Just get on and build it up.

Feed yourself on His truth, and pray in tongues. If that's something you've never done, ask God for the baptism of the Holy Spirit and believe you have received it. Speaking in tongues is then yours. Start to speak and allow this gift to flow. As you feed on God's truth and pray in tongues, your faith will indeed rise and fear will be silenced.

OCTOBER 18TH

<u>Something else to act upon</u>

Keep yourselves in God's love, looking for the mercy of our Lord Jesus Christ to eternal life.
(Jude 1:21)

Jude goes on to tell us to keep ourselves in God's Love. Let me assure you, you can never lose His love. But do you ever feel you've lost the experience of it and feel fearful of what that means? What do you do then? Do you say you need a fresh touch from the Lord? Do you ask God to pour out His love on you again, or ask someone else to pray that prayer for you? Do you wait for God to do something?

God is in you – His touch is on you all the time. He has poured His love out on you; He is pouring His love out on you and He always will pour His love out on you. What more can He do to show you His love and mercy than to sacrifice His own Son just for you and promise you eternal life?

The issue for you isn't that God has stopped loving you – it's that you aren't feeling it. Forget about feelings and go to the truth in His Word. Find verses that tell you of God's love for you. There are lots in this book. Meditate on them and speak them out and keep yourself in the love of God and fear will have to flee.

October 19th

Something to take hold of

"Don't fear what they fear, neither be troubled."
(1 Peter 3:14)

As I write, in the middle of the COVID 19 pandemic, the world is full of fear.

In this verse Peter tells us, as born-again Christians, not to fear what other people fear. With all that's going on, you might think that's impossible. But God never tells us to do something that's impossible. So let's get hold of this – it is possible not to be afraid when everyone else around you is. The question is, how do we do it? The answer is always the same – by standing on the truth of God's Word.

Shut your ears to what the world says: turn the news off, don't go on social media, don't watch films or videos or listen to music that makes you fearful. Do whatever it takes to remove things that might cause you to fear from in front of your eyes and from your ears. Discover God's truth and His promises, meditate on them, choose to believe them, and declare them out loud. It's not an instant fix, but it is a sure one. Stick with it and refuse to budge. When fear is silenced, be wise about how much of the media you let back in. Make sure you hear more positive than negative and more of God than what the world fears.

I'm not telling you how to run your life; I'm explaining the only way to stop fearing what the world fears. It is up to you whether you take hold of it or not. You choose life or death. But let me encourage you as God does, to choose life.

OCTOBER 20TH

Something to decide on

From the end of the earth, I will call to you when my heart is overwhelmed. Lead me to the rock that is higher than I.
(Psalm 61:2)

We know that we should resist the moment fear knocks on our door and silence it with God's Word. But what about the times we don't do that and fear overwhelms us making us feel far away from God's promises?

First let's look at what we don't do. We don't let guilt in on top of the fear; we don't condemn ourselves; we don't hold a pity party; we don't blame God.

So what do we do? We admit we've let fear overwhelm us and receive the forgiveness Jesus has won for us. We turn away from it and do what we know we should have done in the first place. We go to God, not to beg Him to take the fear away, but to take our stand on the unshakeable Rock of Jesus. When we stand on Jesus, we are safe above everything that would try and make us fearful. We replace fear with the Word of God. We declare His truth out loud. We praise Him and thank Him for His love and for all Jesus has done and won for us.

I know from experience that it will probably take longer to silence fear than if we'd resisted it straightaway, but I also know from experience that it will go eventually.

Thank You Jesus that You always have the answer and it is never too late to come to You.

OCTOBER 21ST

Something to declare

Now thanks be to God who always leads us in triumph in Christ.

(2 Corinthians 2:14)

This is another of my favourite verses and what a truth to declare. Jesus has won the victory for us and when we follow Him, He leads us in triumph – He always leads us in triumph. When we are feeling crushed by fear, Jesus is still leading us in triumph. The truth remains no matter what we are feeling. We have to choose what we follow – our feelings or the Word of God.

Are we going to follow our feelings and live defeated by fear, or are we going to follow God's Word and live in triumph? Refuse to listen to any negative feelings and declare out loud, "Thank You Lord God for always leading me in triumph in Christ." See Him leading you in triumph in your imagination.

The more we do this the easier it becomes. Don't get downhearted when you fail, just get back to God's truth and keep feeding yourself with it. God is always leading you in triumph in Jesus. Hallelujah!

OCTOBER 22ND

Something to decide

In the same way, the Spirit also helps our weaknesses, for we don't know how to pray as we ought. But the Spirit himself makes intercession for us with groanings which can't be uttered.

(Romans 8:26)

One of the names for the Holy Spirit is the Helper. How often do we need help and how often do we ask God or the Holy Spirit to help us? It's when we soldier on, trying to work things out for ourselves that problems can arise and fear set in. But we have the Holy Spirit, the Helper, living in us. Let's decide to turn to Him when we need help. Even when we don't know how or even what to ask, He will help us. Thank You Lord.

OCTOBER 23RD

Something to declare

"You shall not be scared of them; for the LORD your God is amongst you, a great and awesome God."

(Deuteronomy 7:21)

This is Moses speaking to the Israelites again before they were to face the battles waiting for them in the Promised Land. Situations and difficulties in your life might seem huge and insurmountable, but you have the great and awesome God on your side. I'll say it again – we have the great and awesome God on our side. Say it out loud – "I have the great and awesome God on my side." What can we possibly fear!

October 24th

Something to put into practice

He said, "If the Syrians are too strong for me, then you shall help me; but if the children of Ammon are too strong for you, then I will come and help you."
(2 Samuel 10:11)

Joab was organising the Israelites to do battle against the people of Ammon and the Syrians. He divided the army into two parts and gave them this instruction to help each other if necessary.

We need to be willing to allow other Christians to help us when we need help – God may have called them to do just that. And we need to be willing to help others as we see their need.

Thank You Lord, that when the battle is on and it is so easy to fear, we can help each other in Your name.

OCTOBER 25TH

Something to act upon

Put on the new man, who in the likeness of God has been created in righteousness and holiness of truth.
(Ephesians 4:24)

We know that, as born-again Christians, we have brand-new, perfect spirits. What we need to do is allow the true nature of God in our spirit to influence and direct our thoughts and our emotions in our soul. We don't need to put the new man on in our spirit – Jesus has already done that. We have the responsibility to put him on in our minds and our hearts. And as we do so, God changes us from glory to glory and fear fades away.

OCTOBER 26TH

Something to remember

For you died, and your life is hidden with Christ in God.
[4] When Christ, our life, is revealed, then you will also be revealed with him in glory.
(Colossians 3:3-4)

What is our human instinct when we are afraid? I think it is to hide. And that is often a good thing to do. If you're confronted by a wild animal, hiding from it will keep you safe. If a storm is about to hit, getting indoors where it can't affect you is a good idea. If someone is out to get you, going somewhere they can't find you is sensible.

But our battle as Christians is against the devil. Where can we go to hide from him? This verse tells us that not only can we hide in Christ, but we are hidden in Christ. When our old nature was put to death with Jesus, our new life became one with Him. Spiritually we are with Him in glory – not waiting to be with Him after we've died, but with Him in glory right now in this life. And when Jesus comes again, that truth will be fully revealed.

When you feel fear, remind yourself that you are hidden in Jesus and there is nothing the devil can do about that – absolutely nothing!

October 27th

Something to know

"Peace I leave with you. My peace I give to you; not as the world gives, I give to you. Don't let your heart be troubled, neither let it be fearful."
(John 14:27)

These are words spoken by Jesus to His disciples the night before He was crucified. They were going to see Him put to death, they were going to suffer persecution throughout their lives and most of them would be put to death for their faith. And Jesus said, "I leave you my peace."

What would they have wanted Him to say – I leave you my courage or my strength? Jesus would indeed give them these things, but first and foremost He wanted them to know that they had His peace.

If we know we have peace with God through Jesus's death and resurrection, then everything else can fall into place. If we doubt that we have peace with God, then fear has a huge wide-open door in our minds and hearts which the devil can easily walk through.

Know for sure that Jesus has given you His peace. He's put it inside you – never doubt it. Don't go trying to get it, or begging God to give it to you. He can't give you what He's already given you. Ask Him to help you to release His peace which is in your spirit, into your mind and heart and play your part by speaking out the truth. That's what will silence fear. Praise Jesus and thank Him for His peace.

October 28th

Something to act upon

Your right hand sustains me.
(Psalm 18:35)

When things are difficult and you feel anxious, it helps to have someone alongside you who you know is able to keep you going and take you through and out the other side of the problem. When a child is scared, what a difference it makes when their mummy or daddy takes hold of their hand.

God's hand is stretched out to us. Let's take hold of it and let Him keep us going, and lead us through and out the other side of the things that we face. Notice that it is His right hand that He offers us. In the Bible, God's right hand signifies His strength and power. And if we hold His right hand, then we are on His righthand side – that's a place of honour. Wow! Can fear remain in the face of that!

Put your hand in His right-hand and let Him sustain you with His strength and power. Thank You Lord.

OCTOBER 29TH

Something to put into practice

For you were once darkness, but are now light in the Lord. Walk as children of light, [9] for the fruit of the Spirit is in all goodness and righteousness and truth, [10] proving what is well pleasing to the Lord.

(Ephesians 5:8-10)

We've talked quite a bit about how we came out of the darkness and into the light of Jesus when we were born-again. Now we need to seek to live our lives in that light. Sometimes we can be tempted to go back to the darkness, even though it no longer has any hold over us. Do we still do things, say things, think things that belong to darkness rather than light? Darkness will always lead to fear. Putting the light on will always dispel the darkness.

Let's decide to live a good life in the righteousness Jesus has won for us and in the truth of all God's Word and fear will have no place. Hallelujah!

October 30th

Something to declare

Christ redeemed us from the curse of the law, having become a curse for us. For it is written, "Cursed is everyone who hangs on a tree."

(Galatians 3:13)

The curse of God came upon everyone who broke any part of the law which He gave to His people in the Old Testament. But because Jesus has won our forgiveness for every sin, past, present and future, we are set free from that curse. He was cursed in our place. What a sacrifice!

This is another of my favourite verses. It's one I declare out loud when fear or guilt tries to condemn me. I refuse to take them on board because Jesus has set me free. Make it your declaration today and turn fear and guilt back with the power of all Jesus has done and won for you through His death and resurrection. The curse is done away with and you are free. Praise Jesus!

OCTOBER 31ST

Something to act upon

Fight the good fight of faith. Take hold of the eternal life to which you were called.

(1 Timothy 6:12)

Does holding on to your faith sometimes feel like a battle? Well it is – the devil would love to rob you of it. But decide to fight the battle, not in your own strength, but by standing on all the truth of God's Word. It's a good fight because, when we stand with Jesus, the victory is already won.

Let's keep going, refusing to let our faith be weakened by fear or anything else and we will indeed know the victory in this life and the next. Hallelujah!

NOVEMBER 1ST

Something to assure you

"Aren't two sparrows sold for an assarion coin? Not one of them falls to the ground apart from your Father's will.
30 But the very hairs of your head are all numbered.
31 Therefore don't be afraid. You are of more value than many sparrows."

(Matthew 10:29-31)

An assarion coin was worth very little. Some Bible versions translate it as a penny. Jesus is making the point that even though these birds are worth so little, God knows when each one dies. And we are of far more value than a sparrow – He even knows how many hairs you have on your head!

Do you fear that God isn't interested in you? That is completely untrue. Know that you are so special to God.

NOVEMBER 2ND

Something to remember

When they had been long without food, Paul stood up in the middle of them and said, "Sirs, you should have listened to me, and not have set sail from Crete and have gotten this injury and loss. 22 Now I exhort you to cheer up, for there will be no loss of life amongst you, but only of the ship. 23 For there stood by me this night an angel, belonging to the God whose I am and whom I serve, 24 saying, 'Don't be afraid, Paul. You must stand before Caesar. Behold, God has granted you all those who sail with you.' 25 Therefore, sirs, cheer up! For I believe God, that it will be just as it has been spoken to me."

(Acts 27:21-25)

Paul had been arrested and was being taken by ship to Rome to be tried before Caesar. On the way they ran into a storm. When it became dangerous, Paul advised the sailors not to continue, but they wouldn't listen and he had to go with them as he was a prisoner. Sometime later, when things looked hopeless, they listened to Paul as he reassured them that they would not drown, even though the ship would be lost. An angel of God had told him this.

Sometimes we can find ourselves in a situation which is not of our own making and beyond our control. But God is still with us and is able to lead us through and out the other side. Instead of panicking, asking "Why me?" and allowing fear in, ask God to show you what to do and how to do it. He will never fail you. He may even use you to help others who are involved in the situation, just as He did with Paul.

NOVEMBER 3RD

Something to declare

Yet I am not ashamed, for I know him whom I have believed, and I am persuaded that he is able to guard that which I have committed to him against that day.
(2 Timothy 1:12)

Paul was saying that nothing could make him ashamed of sharing the gospel, not even persecution. Whatever life throws at you, remember that God is faithful. Never doubt God's faithfulness or ability to bring about what He has promised. Commit yourself to trusting all His promises and all that Jesus has done and won for you and he will bring you through. One day you will be with Him in paradise.

When doubt comes in, don't give in to fear – declare this verse out loud and refuse to be swayed from its truth.

NOVEMBER 4TH

Something to meditate on

When you pass through the waters, I will be with you, and through the rivers, they will not overflow you. When you walk through the fire, you will not be burnt, and flame will not scorch you. [3] For I am the LORD your God, the Holy One of Israel, your Saviour.

(Isaiah 43:2-3)

These are beautiful verses speaking straight to us when we go through really difficult times. If you are facing a huge problem at the moment and finding it hard not to fear, take time to meditate on these verses. Know that if you put your trust in Jesus and God's promises, He will save you. Speak your faith out to silence doubt and fear. Your God, the Holy One of Israel, your Saviour, is on your side and will bring you through. Thank You Lord.

NOVEMBER 5TH

Something to understand

But the wisdom that is from above is first pure, then peaceful, gentle, reasonable, full of mercy and good fruits, without partiality, and without hypocrisy.
(James 3:17)

We have talked a lot about God's wisdom. Here James describes what it is like. Read the list through and thank God for each aspect of His wisdom which He will give you freely when you ask in faith. How can fear stay in the presence of such wonderful wisdom!

NOVEMBER 6TH

Something to put into practice

"You are the light of the world. A city located on a hill can't be hidden. [15] Neither do you light a lamp and put it under a measuring basket, but on a stand; and it shines to all who are in the house. [16] Even so, let your light shine before men, that they may see your good works and glorify your Father who is in heaven."
(Matthew 5:14-16)

Earlier in the year we read that God is the light of the world. Jesus came to the earth as God in the flesh, so it came as no surprise to also read that Jesus is the light of the world. But now Jesus tells us that we are too. How can that be? Jesus lives in us through His Holy Spirit and so His light is in us. He shines as the light of the world through us.

Don't feel fearful and hide it away. Let's be courageous and allow our light to shine so others are drawn to Jesus by how we talk, what we do and how we live our lives.

NOVEMBER 7TH

Something else to put into practice

"You are the salt of the earth".
(Matthew 5:13)

Jesus also told His followers that they were the salt of the earth. Salt has lots of uses – it will preserve food, it will make things taste better, it will kill weeds and it will melt ice.

Are we using our salt or are we hiding it away because we are fearful of what others might think or say? Let's be courageous and go for it with Jesus. Let's preserve God's ways in the way we live, let's make life better for others, let's stand against things that are contrary to God's ways and let's speak the truth of God's love in Jesus to others and see hard hearts melt.

NOVEMBER 8TH

Something to take on board

You came near in the day that I called on you. You said, "Don't be afraid."
(Lamentations 3:57)

God's people had been taken into exile and they were understandably afraid. But they reminded themselves that when they called on God, He told them not to be afraid. God never tells us to do something that's impossible. However difficult it may seem, and it might seem very difficult, it's possible to stop being afraid.

You can try various ways to stop fear and some of them may work for a while, but there is only one way that will deal with fear at its root so you can live your life free from it.

Take hold of God's Word and speak out His promises until fear is silenced. If it comes up again, step in straightaway and attack it with God's truth. Keep going – you will conquer it because Jesus has already won the victory over it for you. Thank You Lord that it's possible not to be afraid.

NOVEMBER 9TH

Something to decide

For, "He who would love life and see good days, let him keep his tongue from evil and his lips from speaking deceit.
[11] Let him turn away from evil and do good. Let him seek peace and pursue it."
(1 Peter 3:10-11)

Peter wrote these verses quoting from Psalm 34. Do you want to love life and see good days? Most of us would say "Yes" to that, though we might mean different things by it. Days which are good in God's eyes are days when we live the way Jesus wants us to out of our love for Him.

So let's be careful what we say and how we say it. Let's speak only God's truth in every situation. Let's make days good for others too. That's the way to find peace instead of fear. Go for it with Jesus helping you every step of the way.

NOVEMBER 10TH

Something to realise

The work of righteousness will be peace, and the effect of righteousness, quietness and confidence forever.
(Isaiah 32:17)

If you are born-again you are righteous – God has made it so. We're told here that the effect of this is peace, quietness and confidence forever. Is that what you are experiencing? Are your mind and heart at peace and quiet or are they filled with fear? Do you have confidence in God or are you full of doubt?

The Bible tells us to be transformed by renewing our minds (Romans 12:2). Know that you are now righteous in your spirit – you are completely right with God – nothing can change that. Let this truth come into your mind and transform you, replacing fear with peace and quietness, and doubt with confidence.

NOVEMBER 11TH

Something to take on board

Then you will prosper, if you observe to do the statutes and the ordinances which the LORD gave Moses concerning Israel. Be strong and courageous. Don't be afraid and don't be dismayed.

(1 Chronicles 22:13)

Many Christians are bothered by the mention of prosperity. Yet God is a generous God who longs to see His children doing well, free from the bondage and fear of poverty and able to bless others. Isn't this what you would want for your children? It's not about living in a huge house with fancy cars and a helicopter thrown in. It's about having more than enough so we are able to live our lives freely with enough money over to support God's work and help others too.

This verse mentions statutes and ordinances. Again, living on this side of Jesus's victory on the Cross, we read this as the Word of God. Love and trust Him and follow His ways. Refuse to be fearful or succumb to despair and you will prosper. Thank You Jesus.

NOVEMBER 12TH

Something to take hold of

"No longer do I call you servants, for the servant doesn't know what his lord does. But I have called you friends, for everything that I heard from my Father, I have made known to you."

(John 15:15)

Jesus spoke these words to His disciples and, as His followers today, we can take hold of them too. Think about it – God Himself calls you His friend. Masters don't take servants into their confidence, but true friends do. And God has shared His whole truth with you through Jesus. He looks on you as His close friend with nothing but love for you.

There's no place for fear within a true friendship – no place for the fear of rejection or betrayal. Know Jesus to be your very best friend and choose to trust Him totally.

NOVEMBER 13TH

<u>Something to decide</u>

I will bless the LORD at all times. His praise will always be in my mouth.
(Psalm 34:1)

Today we are starting to look at the first 10 verses of Psalm 34. It starts with a decision to praise God all the time. You might think you can't praise Him all the time – what about when you need to concentrate on something else?

Make praising God such a part of you that it is always running in the background of your mind and your heart. Take every opportunity you can to thank Him for all the good things in your life. None of us will do this perfectly all the time, but let's set out to do it. The more we do it, the better we will be at it. When we praise and thank God, we bless Him and it lifts our hearts, silencing fear.

NOVEMBER 14TH

Something to put into practice

My soul shall boast in the LORD. The humble shall hear of it and be glad.

(Psalm 34:2)

Your soul is the part of you that thinks and feels and makes decisions. It's your mind, your heart and your decision-making process. Focus them all on God and praise Him for all He has done for you through Jesus. It will lift you out of negative emotions and make you glad. And others, who are willing to hear with their spiritual ears, will be made glad too.

NOVEMBER 15TH

Something to act upon

Oh magnify the LORD with me. Let's exalt his name together.

(Psalm 34:3)

We can't actually magnify God – we can't make Him bigger because He is already infinite. But we can make Him bigger in our thinking. We can't lift Him higher or exalt Him because He is already seated above everything, but we can lift Him up in our thinking. Let's encourage each other to do just that and take the opportunities we can to worship Him together with other true believers. It's a sure way to lift you up out of despair and fear. Magnify Him and exalt Him, and fear will shrink.

NOVEMBER 16TH

Something to remember

I sought the LORD, and he answered me, and delivered me from all my fears.
(Psalm 34:4)

If you find yourself in a situation that could easily overwhelm you with fear, go to God, trust Him to answer you and He will deliver you from all your fears – not just some, but all. The situation may still exist, but as you stand firm with Jesus on all God's promises, the fear of what you're facing will be silenced.

NOVEMBER 17TH

Something to take on board

They looked to him, and were radiant. Their faces shall never be covered with shame.

(Psalm 34:5)

We have the glory of God within us and as we look to Him and praise Him from a sincere heart, His glory will shine on our faces. Wow!

We will never be covered with shame unless we take it on ourselves. If you live in guilt, then you won't see this verse come true for you. I'm not saying that to condemn you, but to encourage you to turn away from guilt and the fear that comes with it. Look to Jesus instead and know that He will never put you to shame – He is always on your side. Cast fear away and let the glory of God radiate from you.

NOVEMBER 18TH

Something to remember

This poor man cried, and the LORD heard him, and saved him out of all his troubles.
(Psalm 34:6)

When you are struggling for some reason, take time to remember all that Jesus has done and won for you and all that God has done in your life in the past. Allow it to lift you up. When we trust Him completely, He will save us out of all our troubles.

NOVEMBER 19TH

Something to realise

The LORD's angel encamps around those who fear him, and delivers them.

(Psalm 34:7)

Do you remember Elisha's servant who saw the army of God's angels around Him when he was terrified of what was going to happen? That army wasn't only around him; it is around you today when you fear God, that is respect Him and hold Him in awe.

In your mind imagine the angels encamped around you and choose to believe that they will deliver you. That's the instruction they have from God. He doesn't want you terrified and, through Jesus, He has already won the victory for every situation you face. Thank You Lord.

NOVEMBER 20TH

Something to act upon

Oh taste and see that the LORD is good.
(Psalm 34:8)

Lots of people deny that there is a God. Some do believe there must be a superior being, but reject Jesus. Some have accepted Jesus, but never really take hold of the victory He has won for them. These people are refusing to taste who God is and all He has done through Jesus. Then they wonder why they are prone to fear and discouragement.

Let me encourage you to taste the truth of God in His Word and you will indeed see that the Lord is good.

NOVEMBER 21ST

Something to understand

Blessed is the man who takes refuge in him.
(Psalm 34:8)

Do you want to be blessed? I'm guessing your answer is "Yes." Then take refuge in God. Trust Him to protect you and lead you through and out of your problems. Don't look to your own ideas or what the world says – that's the way to doubt and fear. Go to God, trusting Him completely, and you will be blessed and kept safe from the enemy.

NOVEMBER 22ND

Something to take hold of

Oh fear the LORD, you his saints, for there is no lack with those who fear him.

(Psalm 34:9)

Here is another prosperity verse. If you don't believe in God's prosperity, then you will have to cut this verse out of your Bible! How much time do we spend worrying about things we need but don't have? We have to take our eyes off our needs and look to God with respect and awe. Trust Him and He will give you more than enough. Praise Him!

NOVEMBER 23RD

Something more to take hold of

The young lions do lack, and suffer hunger, but those who seek the LORD shall not lack any good thing.
(Psalm 34:10)

This emphasises what we said yesterday. We may see others going hungry and living in need, but when our focus is truly on God and we are trusting His promises which are all stamped 'yes' by Jesus, then we have nothing to fear. We shall not lack any good thing. And we are then able to help others. Hallelujah!

NOVEMBER 24TH

Something to determine

"Don't be afraid of those who kill the body, but are not able to kill the soul. Rather, fear him who is able to destroy both soul and body in Gehenna."
(Matthew 10:28)

This is something quite hard to get your head around and just reading this verse can make you feel fearful. But resist that and let's look at exactly what it says.

Jesus says not to fear those who kill the body. The only way we can possibly not be afraid when someone is threatening to kill us is to know for certain where we are going when we die. If we have any doubt, then fear will strike.

Do you know for sure that you are going to heaven? Because the only alternative is Gehenna or hell. God doesn't want anyone to go to hell, but He can't have people who reject Jesus in heaven. Jesus is the way to heaven, so if you have rejected Him you've rejected the way to get there. But if you fear God, that is respect Him and hold Him in awe, then you will want to learn from His Word and accept the sacrifice of Jesus for your forgiveness and salvation. And then you will be on your way to heaven – no question.

Don't give fear the victory. Feed yourself on the truth of God's Word and know for certain that you will be in heaven with Jesus one day, so even the threat of death will not cause you to fear. Hallelujah!

NOVEMBER 25TH

Something to grasp

In this, love has been made perfect amongst us, that we may have boldness in the day of judgement, because as he is, even so we are in this world.

(1 John 4:17)

We come to another of my favourite verses. There will be a day of judgement one day, but the judgement will be about whether we have accepted Jesus as our Lord and Saviour or not. It won't be about all our sins, just that one thing. So there will be no punishment for us as born-again Christians – we can contemplate the day of judgement with boldness because of the perfect love of Jesus who died in our place.

Not only this, but look at how this verse ends. It says we are like Jesus. Not that we will be one day, but that we are now in this world! How can that be? In our spirit we are perfect – it is merged with the Holy Spirit to form one spirit which is as perfect now as it ever will be for eternity. That's so amazing. That should silence fear. Thank You Jesus that as You are, even so am I in this world.

NOVEMBER 26TH

Something to put into practice

"Listen, all Judah, and you inhabitants of Jerusalem, and you, king Jehoshaphat. The LORD says to you, 'Don't be afraid, and don't be dismayed because of this great multitude; for the battle is not yours, but God's.
16 Tomorrow, go down against them. Behold, they are coming up by the ascent of Ziz. You will find them at the end of the valley, before the wilderness of Jeruel.
17 You will not need to fight this battle. Set yourselves, stand still, and see the salvation of the LORD with you, O Judah and Jerusalem. Don't be afraid, nor be dismayed. Go out against them tomorrow, for the LORD is with you."
(2 Chronicles 20:15-17)

Once again, we have instructions before a battle in the Old Testament. This time Jahaziel is speaking. He tells the people that the battle isn't theirs, but God's. Remember, our enemy is not the people involved, but the devil. So when we know that we are fighting on God's side, then we can be assured that the battle isn't ours but His.

Our part is to set ourselves in the truth of God's Word and stand firm in it. Then we will see the battle won. Know that God is always with you and refuse to fear. Jesus has already won the victory.

NOVEMBER 27TH

Something to act upon

All chastening seems for the present to be not joyous but grievous; yet afterward it yields the peaceful fruit of righteousness to those who have been trained by it.
12 Therefore lift up the hands that hang down and the
feeble knees, 13 and make straight paths for your feet, so
what is lame may not be dislocated, but rather be healed.

(Hebrews 12:11-13)

God will discipline us when we have strayed from His ways and aren't recognising that we need to turn back. He always uses His Word either directly or through someone else. But He never does it in anger – it is always done in love. It's to encourage us to live His way for our own sake. He's not angry and it's not about punishment – all our sins have already been punished on the Cross and our forgiveness has been won. Never think that sickness or hardship is God punishing you – it's not. Remember John 10:10? If it's bad, it's from the devil; if it's good, it's from God.

Don't let yourself buckle under it when God disciplines you. And don't condemn yourself. Understand what He's saying and rejoice because you know it's only done out of love for your benefit. His burden is light and turning back to God's way always brings peace. And where there is God's peace, fear has no place.

So listen to what God is saying to you and walk forward on the straight path He has set before you, confident in His unconditional love for you. What He wants for you is that you are able to function fully and not be crippled and limited by failure. Rejoice that He loves you enough to set you right.

NOVEMBER 28TH

Something to determine

I have learnt in whatever state I am, to be content in it. [12] I know how to be humbled, and I also know how to abound. In any and all circumstances I have learnt the secret both to be filled and to be hungry, both to abound and to be in need.

(Philippians 4:11-12)

Paul reached a place where he could be content in any and every situation he found himself in, be it good or bad. That's quite something. It's a place where peace rules, not fear. How did he do it? There is no shortcut – it's trusting Jesus more and more and looking to God's Word above everything else. We may not have got to that place yet, but let's determine to be on the journey towards it and keep moving forward. God is with us.

NOVEMBER 29TH

Something to remember

When evening had come, the boat was in the middle of the sea, and he was alone on the land. [48] Seeing them distressed in rowing, for the wind was contrary to them, about the fourth watch of the night he came to them, walking on the sea; and he would have passed by them. [49] but they, when they saw him walking on the sea, supposed that it was a ghost, and cried out; [50] for they all saw him and were troubled. But he immediately spoke with them and said to them, "Cheer up! It is I! Don't be afraid." [51] He got into the boat with them; and the wind ceased, and they were very amazed amongst themselves, and marvelled.

(Mark 6:47-51)

Once again, the disciples were in a boat being tossed about by a violent storm. Jesus saw they were in trouble and came to them walking on the water. But He does something which you might not expect – He continues walking on as if to go past the boat! The disciples see Him and, although they are frightened and think He is a ghost, they cry out to Him. Jesus then comes to them, telling them to cheer up and not be afraid. He stills the storm and the disciples are amazed and marvel at Him.

God hasn't promised to just step in and sort everything out when we get into difficulty. He wants us to use the faith He has given us to call to Him for help. Don't let fear blind you to the help that is there ready for you. Cry out to God. He is faithful and when you reach out in faith, He will always respond. We marvel at your love and power, Lord Jesus.

NOVEMBER 30TH

Something to look forward to

"You men of Galilee, why do you stand looking into the sky? This Jesus, who was received up from you into the sky, will come back in the same way as you saw him going into the sky."

(Acts 1:11)

After the disciples had watched Jesus be taken up into heaven in a cloud, I can imagine them just standing there, staring and staring at the sky. An angel spoke to them and reassured them that one day Jesus would return again in just the same way. We are still waiting for His return, but we wait in the certain knowledge that the day will come and when He does come back, He will come in glory.

We live in a world in turmoil and full of fear, but when Jesus returns, everything will be sorted out according to God's perfect plan. It is something to look forward to and anticipating it will silence fear.

December 1st

Something to put into practice

The righteous will be remembered forever. [7] He will not be afraid of evil news. His heart is steadfast, trusting in the LORD. [8] His heart is established. He will not be afraid in the end when he sees his adversaries.

(Psalm 112:6-8)

Because we have accepted Jesus as our Lord and Saviour, we are made righteous through His victory on the Cross, and we will never be forgotten by God. Don't let fear tell you otherwise.

As God's children, we do not need to fear bad news. Let's keep our hearts steadfast, trusting the Lord. That is what will establish our hearts, and an established heart will not be shaken. Even when the devil tries to come against us, we can stand fearlessly, strong and safe in Jesus.

December 2nd

Something to meditate on

Since then the children have shared in flesh and blood, he also himself in the same way partook of the same, that through death he might bring to nothing him who had the power of death, that is, the devil, [15] and might deliver all of them who through fear of death were all their lifetime subject to bondage.

(Hebrews 2:14-15)

Are you frightened of death? It's understandable if you think this is the only life there is. But that kind of fear will keep you in bondage because, unless Jesus returns first, there is no escaping death.

Jesus became a man so that He could die too, but in so doing He won the victory over death for you and for me. The devil no longer has the power of death. Jesus defeated it when He came back from the dead, and when we put our trust in Him, we will do so too. Think about it, meditate on it and let it settle in your heart. It will set you free from the fear of death if you will let it.

December 3rd

Something to look forward to

Behold, I tell you a mystery. We will not all sleep, but we
will all be changed, 52 in a moment, in the twinkling of an
eye, at the last trumpet. For the trumpet will sound and
the dead will be raised incorruptible, and we will be
changed. 53 For this perishable body must become
imperishable, and this mortal must put on immortality.
54 But when this perishable body will have become
imperishable, and this mortal will have put on immortality,
then what is written will happen: "Death is swallowed up
in victory." 55 "Death, where is your sting? Hades, where is
your victory?"
(1 Corinthians 15:51-55)

As a born-again believer, this is what will happen to you when you die. Knowing this robs death of its power over your thoughts and emotions. Instead of fearing it, it is something amazing to look forward to!

December 4th

Something to understand

For whatever is born of God overcomes the world. This is the victory that has overcome the world: your faith. [5] Who is he who overcomes the world, but he who believes that Jesus is the Son of God?

(1 John 5:4-5)

How we long to overcome the troubles of this world with all its fears. How we long to have the victory. Well, it's ours for the taking. Put your faith in Jesus and all He has done and won for you, and you will be able to overcome fear and every negative emotion. Why? Because you are putting your faith in the very Son of God. You are an overcomer. Believe it and you will find it's true.

DECEMBER 5TH

Something to take on board

She said, "As the LORD your God lives, I don't have anything baked, but only a handful of meal in a jar and a little oil in a jar. Behold, I am gathering two sticks, that I may go in and bake it for me and my son, that we may eat it, and die." [13] Elijah said to her, "Don't be afraid. Go and do as you have said; but make me a little cake from it first, and bring it out to me, and afterward make some for you and for your son. [14] For the LORD, the God of Israel, says, 'The jar of meal will not run out, and the jar of oil will not fail, until the day that the LORD sends rain on the earth.' " [15] She went and did according to the saying of Elijah; and she, he, and her household ate many days. [16] The jar of meal didn't run out and the jar of oil didn't fail, according to the LORD's word, which he spoke by Elijah.

(1 Kings 17:12-16)

This is an amazing story about Elijah and a widow who had only enough food left for one last meal for herself and her son. It hadn't rained for a long time and there was a shortage of food in the land. Elijah came along and asked her to make a small meal for him first. Elijah then told her that if she did this, she would not run out of food. Instead of reacting negatively to Elijah's request, the woman did as he asked and her store of food kept multiplying until it rained again and more food could be grown again.

Sometimes God asks us to do something which doesn't seem to make sense. Be sure it is God who is directing you, and then choose to obey him. Fear comes from trying to do things our way. Peace comes from doing them God's way.

December 6th

Something to take on board

But the fruit of the Spirit is love, joy, peace, patience, kindness, goodness, faith, [23] gentleness, and self-control. Against such things there is no law.
(Galatians 5:22-23)

We have the Holy Spirit living in us. Just pause a moment and really take that on board. If you are born-again, you have the Holy Spirit living in you, and He is in you in His fullness, with all His attributes listed in these verses.

You're probably thinking, "But I'm not always loving and joyful. I don't always show peace, patience, kindness, goodness, faithfulness, gentleness or self-control." No, none of us do. But we have to remember that the Holy Spirit lives in our perfect spirit, which was given to us when we became true believers. In our spirit all the fruit of the Spirit lives perfectly mature. We need to allow it to flow into our minds and hearts so it can influence what we think and say and do.

Do you worry about your attitudes and reactions? Don't ask God to give you His fruit – He can't give you what He's already given you. Take on board that the fruit is in you, fully formed and ripe. No-one can ever take it away from you, no matter what they do. No law can ever be passed that could take the fruit of the Spirit from you. Let that settle in your thinking. Go to His Word and feed on His truth. Ask Him to help you day by day to make decisions and act according to what is in your spirit. You will find that the fruit will start to be more and more evident in your life and fear will have less and less of a place.

December 7th

Something to decide

Listen, my son, and receive my sayings. The years of your life will be many.
(Proverbs 4:10)

Do you remember when we read that God's Word is health to your body? Well, if we are healthy, the consequence is that we will live longer. We know there are other factors involved as well to do with the way we live, but do not underestimate the power of God's Word. Yes, look after your body, but don't let the fear of ill health take over your life. Decide to take God at His word. Believe and receive the sayings of God and you will live for many years.

December 8th

Something to know

For I reckon that the sufferings of this present time are not worthy to be compared with the glory which shall be revealed in us.

(Romans 8:18 KJV)

When things are difficult and you are feeling fearful, take your eyes off what you're going through and focus on where you're going to – living with Jesus in glory! Look again at this verse. When we get to heaven the glory of God isn't going to be revealed to us, but in us. Yes, it's already in you. Wow!

Dwell on that when things are hard. Don't waste time thinking that you can't see it or feel it. No, just believe it and thank God for it. Thank You Jesus for your glory in me. Fear, you cannot stand in the face of the glory of God in me. Praise you Lord. Amen.

DECEMBER 9TH

Something to take on board

"I will in no way leave you, neither will I in any way forsake you."

(Hebrews 13:5)

This is the promise of the Almighty God for you. He will never, ever leave you; He will never, ever forsake you. Don't start to fear if you aren't feeling the presence of God. Thank Him each day that He is with you, whether you feel it or not. Feelings aren't important – they won't set you free from fear, but the truth of God will.

December 10th

Something to decide

"But whoever listens to me will dwell securely, and will be at ease, without fear of harm."

(Proverbs 1:33)

We either fear about the consequences of something that has already happened or about the consequences of something that might happen. God promises us that if we trust Him in His Word, then we do not need to fear, whatever happens. You can refuse to believe this and discuss it endlessly with other people, but in the end it is true, because God has said it. Decide to trust Him in this – only then will you find that it is indeed true.

DECEMBER 11TH

Something to encourage you

"The Spirit of the Lord is on me, because he has anointed me to preach good news to the poor. He has sent me to heal the broken hearted, to proclaim release to the captives, recovering of sight to the blind, to deliver those who are crushed, [19] and to proclaim the acceptable year of the Lord."

(Luke 4:18-19)

These are the words of Jesus explaining what He had come to earth to do. Read through this list again slowly. Each one can deal with fear.

If you are fearful because you have nothing and see no way forward, then know that Jesus has good news for you – salvation through Him. If you are fearful because you have a broken heart, then know that Jesus wants to heal you. If you are fearful because you are held captive in some way in your thinking or in your habits, then know that Jesus wants to set you free. If you are fearful because you are either physically or spiritually blind, then know that Jesus wants to give you your sight. If you are fearful because you have been crushed by life, then know that Jesus wants to deliver you from under that weight.

Jesus proclaimed the acceptable year of the Lord. Through His death and resurrection, He has made everyone who will believe in Him acceptable to God. So take hold of all Jesus wants to do in you and for you. He's already done it in the spiritual realm. Receive it by faith and be set free from fear.

DECEMBER 12TH

<u>Something to determine</u>

For you have been a stronghold to the poor, a stronghold to the needy in his distress, a refuge from the storm, a shade from the heat, when the blast of the dreaded ones is like a storm against the wall.

(Isaiah 25:4)

When a storm hits, let's go to God in His Word. He will keep us safe when we trust in Him. Even when things rage against us, trying to batter us down, let's determine not to fear but to go to the Lord. He is the only One who can truly protect us and save us.

DECEMBER 13TH

Something to rejoice about

He hath made us accepted in the beloved.
(Ephesians 1:6 KJV)

Jesus is God's' beloved Son. Because of all that Jesus did and won for us through His death and resurrection, we are accepted by God. If you have experienced rejection or fear it, let this soak deep into your heart. Let it still your fear and comfort you. You are accepted by God just as you are. Thank You, thank You Jesus.

December 14th

Something to understand

They overcame him because of the Lamb's blood, and because of the word of their testimony.
(Revelation 12:11)

When we put our trust in Jesus and accept him as our Lord and Saviour, we become overcomers. In Jesus we can overcome anything and everything that would try to come against us, including fear. We may not feel like overcomers or act like overcomers, but overcomers we are. We don't deserve to be and we can't earn the right to be – it is only because Jesus shed His blood for us that we are.

This verse gives us further insight into being an overcomer. It says we overcome the world by the word of our testimony as well. There is power in sharing your faith with others, in telling them of all Jesus has done in your life. Use God's wisdom when and how to do this, but let's decide to share the Good News of Jesus with others and live as the overcomers we truly are.

December 15th

Something to encourage you

But you followed my teaching, conduct, purpose, faith, patience, love, steadfastness, [11] persecutions, and sufferings — those things that happened to me at Antioch, Iconium, and Lystra. I endured those persecutions. The Lord delivered me out of them all.

(2 Timothy 3:10-11)

Paul is writing to Timothy, a young church leader. He reminds him of his teaching and of the persecutions that he suffered in different places. And he encourages him by telling him that God delivered him out of them all.

Thank You Lord that You will deliver me out of everything I face in your name. Even if it came to death, You will deliver me into an eternity of love, joy and peace with You. I have nothing to fear. Thank You Lord.

December 16th

Something to assure you

For by grace you have been saved through faith, and that not of yourselves; it is the gift of God, [9] not of works, that no one would boast.

(Ephesians 2:8-9)

As we come towards the end of the year, it's good to remind ourselves of the basis of our salvation. We could never have achieved it by our own effort – it came to us as a free gift from God. It is by grace that we have been saved. But we did have a part to play – we had to receive God's free gift through faith in Jesus and all He had done and won for us. (I have used that phrase a lot – I love it!)

Don't let fear tell you you're not good enough. It has nothing to do with how good or bad we are. It's all about God's grace and our response in faith. Thank You Lord!

December 17th

Something to declare

Grace, mercy, and peace will be with us, from God the Father and from the Lord Jesus Christ, the Son of the Father, in truth and love.

(2 John 1:3)

God's grace is with us all the time – His unconditional love poured out on us regardless of the fact that we don't deserve it and could never earn it. And it is the same with His peace. You may not be feeling God's love or His peace, but get hold of this – they are with you.

When fear tries to tell you that God can't possible love you and peace seems miles away, declare this verse out loud. It is truth and it comes to you from your loving Father and from your Lord and Saviour, Jesus Christ. Fear will be silenced when we know, regardless of our feelings, that we live in a love relationship with God and declare our trust in Him.

Say, "Grace, mercy, and peace are with me, from God my Father and from my Lord Jesus Christ, the Son of my Father, in truth and love."

December 18th

Something to act upon

Therefore Jesus did many other signs in the presence of his disciples, which are not written in this book; [31] but these are written that you may believe that Jesus is the Christ, the Son of God, and that believing you may have life in his name.

(John 20:30-31)

God inspired people to write down the truth of who Jesus is and what He said and did, so we could know that He is indeed the Son of God, and have eternal life with Him if we believe.

If you've come this far reading this book and still have not accepted Jesus as your Lord and Saviour, then go back to January 5th and do so today. You will be on the way to defeating fear in your life as you put your trust in Him and Him alone.

DECEMBER 19TH

Something to look forward to

But, according to his promise, we look for new heavens and a new earth, in which righteousness dwells.
(2 Peter 3:13)

God has promised us new heavens and a new earth. He has told us that one day we will reign with Him when He returns in glory. Our life will be so amazing, beyond anything we can begin to imagine.

When the troubles of this world are getting you down and fear is knocking at the door, lift your eyes and your thoughts to what is to come and praise your God. When we are living for eternity in glory with Jesus, we will have no thought for what happened down here. Spend today with that thought and fear won't have opportunity to make itself heard.

December 20th

Something to lift you

"For you shall go out with joy, and be led out with peace. The mountains and the hills will break out before you into singing; and all the trees of the fields will clap their hands."
(Isaiah 55:12)

The Bible tells us that all of creation is groaning, waiting for the day when everything is put right and made perfect. But the Bible also tells us that even in this broken world, creation is singing praises to God.

Instead of sinking beneath the weight of all that is happening and the fear that threatens, let's join with nature and sing God's praises. Let's go out with joy and allow God's peace to lead us. Let's lift our voices and clap our hands in praise to our God, and fear will indeed be silenced.

December 21st

Something to understand

The Word became flesh and lived amongst us. We saw his glory, such glory as of the only born Son of the Father, full of grace and truth.

(John 1:14)

Today we start to look at some verses to do with Christmas – the birth of Jesus. Earlier in his gospel, John explains that Jesus is the very Word of God. I've said so much about God's Word in this book. Now we find that Jesus is the Word itself in the flesh. He wasn't just a baby to sing carols about. He always has been, is and will always be the Son of God, full of glory and grace and truth.

Today, we don't see Him in the flesh; we believe in Him through faith. He is now seated in glory with God the Father and living in us by His Holy Spirit. We have the glory and grace and truth of Jesus living in us. How can we possibly fear!

December 22nd

Something to decide

"Blessed is she who believed, for there will be a fulfilment of the things which have been spoken to her from the Lord!"

(Luke 1:45)

These are words spoken by Mary's cousin, Elizabeth, when she first saw Mary pregnant with Jesus. I love this verse. Mary believed God when the angel told her she would give birth to His Son, and because she had believed, Elizabeth declared under God's inspiration that it would come to pass.

Decide today to believe what God says to you in His Word and through His Holy Spirit. When you believe and do not doubt, then it will come about and you will be blessed. Don't be afraid – God is good and only wants to do good things in your life.

DECEMBER 23RD

Something to determine

But when he thought about these things, behold, an angel of the Lord appeared to him in a dream, saying, "Joseph, son of David, don't be afraid to take to yourself Mary as your wife, for that which is conceived in her is of the Holy Spirit."

(Matthew 1:20)

Joseph was betrothed to Mary, which was a binding commitment in those days. When he realised Mary was having a baby and he knew it couldn't be his, we can imagine the thoughts that went through his head – thoughts of anger and hurt and fear. By Jewish law he was justified in having her stoned to death, but he still loved Mary so he decided to send her away quietly.

However, after he had made that decision, God sent an angel to him in a dream who reassured him that Mary hadn't been unfaithful to him, but was carrying the Son of God. Joseph didn't spend any time querying this or doubting it. He took God at His Word and stood by Mary in faith.

I think Joseph is a wonderful example to us all. Things may seem confusing and the outlook might look bleak, but take God at His Word. Choose to cast fearful thoughts away and believe what God says, not what the world says or your own feelings say. Let's determine to always go God's way in faith.

DECEMBER 24TH

Something to rejoice about

There were shepherds in the same country staying in the field, and keeping watch by night over their flock. [9] Behold, an angel of the Lord stood by them, and the glory of the Lord shone around them, and they were terrified. [10] The angel said to them, "Don't be afraid, for behold, I bring you good news of great joy which will be to all the people.
[11] For there is born to you today, in David's city, a Saviour, who is Christ the Lord."

(Luke 2:8-11)

Who would you choose to announce the birth of God to? Maybe royalty or the government of the country or the leaders of the Jewish faith? God chose some shepherds living with their sheep in the fields. They weren't important in the world's eyes; they probably didn't have a lot of education, if any; and they would be unclean and smelly living and dealing with sheep up in the hills. Let that speak to you. You can never be unimportant to God, no matter what you've done or whatever your situation is. God wants you to know the truth of His love for you.

Suddenly an angel appeared to the shepherds and the sky shone with the glory of God. Unsurprisingly they were afraid. But the angel told them not to fear and gave them the best news in the world – their Saviour had been born.

Don't be afraid when God speaks to you through His Word or His Holy Spirit. Listen to what He is saying and rejoice at the wonderful news of Jesus your Saviour, who was born and died and was resurrected for you, so you could spend eternity with Him.

December 25th

Something to know

"Glory to God in the highest, on earth peace, good will towards men."

(Luke 2:14)

Then many other angels joined the first and they sang praises to God. They declared peace on earth. They didn't mean peace between people, but peace between people and God. Jesus was going to win that peace by taking the punishment for our sins so we wouldn't have to suffer it ourselves.

Know that God has only good will towards you, never bad. Put away fear and doubt, and rejoice in your good God who loves you so much that He sent His own Son to this earth to live and die for you so you could be at peace with Him. Glory to God!

December 26th

Something to take on board

For a child is born to us. A son is given to us; and the government will be on his shoulders. His name will be called Wonderful Counsellor, Mighty God, Everlasting Father, Prince of Peace.

(Isaiah 9:6)

Seven hundred years before Jesus was born as a baby here on earth, Isaiah prophesied that it would happen. God showed him some of the names of Jesus. Let's look at each one.

'Wonderful Counsellor' – the one to whom we can always turn when we don't know what to do. 'Mighty God' – God Himself born to live and die for us. 'Everlasting Father' – the perfect Father who will never, ever leave us or forsake us. 'Prince of Peace' – the only One who could pay the price for our sins so we could be at peace with God and know Him as our Father.

Spend some time meditating on these names and allow them to quieten your fears.

DECEMBER 27TH

Something to reassure you

"You afflicted, tossed with storms, and not comforted, behold, I will set your stones in beautiful colours, and lay your foundations with sapphires. [12] I will make your pinnacles of rubies, your gates of sparkling jewels, and all your walls of precious stones."

(Isaiah 54:11-12)

Here Isaiah is comparing God's people to a city that has been devastated by a storm. If you've been through a very difficult time and you feel battered and bruised, know that God isn't going to rebuild you with rubble. No, He's going to rebuild you with beautiful, precious stones that sparkle but which are enduring.

When fear tries to strike, use your imagination and see yourself rebuilt with the most precious of stones. Take your eyes off the problem and sparkle for Him, knowing that those stones can never be destroyed.

December 28th

Something to determine

It is because of The LORD's loving kindnesses that we are not consumed, because his mercies don't fail. [23] They are new every morning. Great is your faithfulness.
(Lamentations 3:22-23)

This was written when God's people were in exile. Life wasn't the way they wanted it to be, but instead of grumbling and feeling anxious, they put their focus on God and all His goodness. Living this side of the Cross we know that it is God's love shown to us through Jesus that stops us from being overwhelmed by circumstances and fear. Dwell on that when times get tough, and you will find it is true.

When you're in a situation you don't want to be in, turn to the Lord and praise Him for His loving-kindness towards you. That hasn't changed and never will. His mercy wasn't given you just for when life was running smoothly, but for every single day, no matter what is happening. His mercy will never fail. Each morning God's mercies are as new and active as they were the day before. God is faithful and He will never let you down.

When you wake in the morning, before despair and fear can get a hold, determine to thank God for His loving-kindness, and His mercies. Praise Him for His faithfulness.

DECEMBER 29TH

Something to declare

For you didn't receive the spirit of bondage again to fear, but you received the Spirit of adoption, by whom we cry, "Abba! Father!"

(Romans 8:15)

We are coming to the end of the year. I trust you have been helped and encouraged to step out confidently with Jesus. Here, Paul reminds us that once we have been set free, we need to be careful not to allow fear back in. God never puts fear on us. Instead He has made us His own children and brought us into His family. We can call Almighty God, Daddy! What a wonderful thought!

If fear tries to come back, banish it with these words. Declare out loud with authority, "I didn't receive the spirit of bondage again to fear, but I received the Spirit of adoption, by whom I cry, "Abba! Father! Daddy!"

December 30th

Something to decide

Finally, be strong in the Lord and in the strength of his might.

(Ephesians 6:10)

We have covered so much through this book of the truth of God. I encourage you now to make a decision to go forward in the strength of the Lord, able to recognise the devil's tactics when he tries them on, and knowing how to resist him and the fear he tries to bring.

Yes, you can be strong in the strength of God's power and might. Go for it!

DECEMBER 31ST

Something to do

You are my God, and I will give thanks to you. You are my God, I will exalt you. [29] Oh give thanks to the LORD, for he is good, for his loving kindness endures forever.
(Psalm 118:28-29)

Let's finish the year with thanks to our God. Let's lift Him up in our thinking and in our hearts for He is good and His loving-kindness endures for ever. Amen.

At the End of the Year

We have come to the end of the year. I trust you have found this book helpful and encouraging. There's no reason why you shouldn't go back to the beginning and start again. But whatever you do, keep reminding yourself of what you have read from God's Word. When you are tempted to fear, before it has time to take hold, replace it with His truth. Allow His Word to settle deeper and deeper into your thinking and your emotions, creating an increasingly strong basis for your faith.

Don't get down if you still find conquering fear difficult, and don't give up. Remember, the more you do it, the easier it becomes. Be assured that, because of Jesus, it is possible to silence fear when it tries to rise up. You have the ultimate weapon in your hand – the sword of the Spirit which is the Word of God. Walk forward boldly into the next year with Jesus, secure in the truth that you are an overcomer. Praise the Lord!

Thanks be to God, who gives us the victory through our Lord Jesus Christ.
(1 Corinthians 15:57)

Bible Passage Index

Understanding Christianity

To find more by Katherine Hilditch go to –

UnderstandingChristianity.co.uk

where you can read, download and print out all her booklets completely free of charge

Titles include –

Spirit, Soul and Body
Praying for Others
God Loves You
Who is the Holy Spirit?
God Wants You to Be Well
Praying for Yourself
God's Not Angry With You
Be Transformed
Forgiveness
Psalm 91

Printed in Great Britain
by Amazon

50494571R00217